PRAISE

Wow! Mary Jo's compelling story grabbed me on the first page. Heartbreaking, poignant, and real, she shares the brutal truth about the "gray divorce." But she also offers humor, hope, and lots of practical advice for emotional and spiritual healing.

ROSE SWEET – Catholic Author and Speaker

❖ ❖ ❖

A must read for every woman whose entire world has been shattered by going through a divorce. This book is a true message of hope that will help you see who *you are through the eyes of* whose *you are.*

CONNIE WETZELL – Author, Speaker, and Voice Artist

❖ ❖ ❖

Mary Jo's raw and deeply vulnerable personal account of her husband's shocking infidelity and her journey back to wholeness will be a source of strength and healing for many women worldwide. If you or someone you know has experienced betrayal and divorce, I highly recommend you read this book. It will transform your life!

APRIL YVETTE – Motivational Speaker and Purpose-Driven Sales Expert

YOU ARE STILL BELOVED

YOU ARE STILL BELOVED

When Your Long-Term Marriage Ends in Divorce

MARY JO RENNERT

Stonebrook Publishing
Saint Louis, Missouri

A STONEBROOK PUBLISHING BOOK
© 2020 Mary Jo Rennert

All rights reserved. Published in the United States by Stonebrook Publishing, a division of Stonebrook Enterprises, LLC, Saint Louis, Missouri. No part of this book may be reproduced, scanned, or distributed in any printed or electronic form without written permission from the author. Please do not participate in or encourage piracy of copyrighted materials in violation of the author's rights.

Scripture texts are taken from the *New American Bible, revised edition* © 2010, 1991, 1986, 1970 Confraternity of Christian Doctrine, Washington, D.C. and are used by permission of the copyright owner. All Rights Reserved. No part of the New American Bible may be reproduced in any form without permission in writing from the copyright owner.

Author photo by Michael Durr Photo/Video, LLC

Library of Congress Control Number: 2020909184
ISBN: 978-1-7347340-1-0

www.stonebrookpublishing.net

PRINTED IN THE UNITED STATES OF AMERICA

10 9 8 7 6 5 4 3 2 1

*For all those who journey
through the dark night of divorce—*

May this book help light your way.

CONTENTS

1: The Phone Call	1
2: Recognizing Who Did What to Whom	13
3: Surviving the Unthinkable	15
4: Coping with Emotional Overload	19
5: Battling Fear and Worry	23
6: Grieving Many Losses	31
7: Making Healthy Choices	39
8: Dealing with Family and Friends	43
9: Relieving Spiritual and Creative Dryness	51
10: Acquiring Power Tools	59
11: Encountering Setbacks	63
12: Coping with Isolation, Loneliness, and Loss of Identity	71
13: Keeping Your Guard Up	81
14: Learning to Forgive	87
15: Becoming the Person God Created You to Be	95
16: Letting God's Love Shine Through You	99
17: Seeking Continuous Improvement	103
Fifteen Actions to Help You Move from Broken to Whole	107
Acknowledgments	109
About the Author	111

For it is not an enemy that reviled me—
that I could bear—
Not a foe who viewed me with contempt,
from that I could hide.

But it was you, my other self,
my comrade and friend,
You, whose company I enjoyed,
at whose side I walked
in the house of God.

Psalm 55:13–15

Chapter 1

THE PHONE CALL

"MARY, CALL ME back right away. It's about your husband. It's an emergency."

I listened to the voicemail twice to make sure I'd understood it. The caller ID showed an out-of-state area code. I figured maybe it was a scam, but these days, a lot of local people have different area codes. It didn't occur to me to call my husband first. The word *emergency* conjured up all kinds of images, none of them comforting, so I took a deep breath and punched in the numbers. Not on my cell phone, though. This person had called my office phone. That was odd, but the female caller could have found me on LinkedIn or by Google search. She'd recognize that number rather than my cell.

And she'd called me *Mary*, not *Mary Jo*, which meant she didn't know me. Only two friends in my sixty-four years had called me Mary: one from grade school, the other from high school. No, this woman must be a stranger. Perhaps my husband had been in an accident, and a Good Samaritan had called to let me know. The call had come in two hours earlier, while I'd spent the morning in meetings. The delay now added to my sense of urgency.

"Hello?" The woman on the other end hesitated. She sounded young.

"I received a message from this number about some kind of emergency." I could hear the concern in my voice, but I tried to sound professional.

"Mary, are you sure you want to talk to me while you're at work? I have something very important to tell you."

I assured her that if it was an emergency, I certainly did want to know, and by the way, who was she?

"My name's Kiana, and I'm having an affair with your husband."

I didn't see that coming. "Really? I doubt that."

My husband owned several investment properties, and I figured this was probably a disgruntled renter he was trying to evict.

"I live in one of your rental houses. I know all about you. I know you have two children, that they're adopted, that you couldn't have any children yourself. I've seen pictures of you and photos of your vacation when you both went out to see your daughter. The ones where you were hiking in the forest with the big trees."

Last June. Olympic National Park in Washington. I'm not very active on Facebook, so I couldn't fluff her off as someone who gleaned that information from social media. She must at least know someone close to us to have that knowledge.

Her voice quickened. Now that she had my attention, it was as if this woman needed to unburden her soul.

"I've been to your house. I've seen your guest bedroom. I know how your kitchen's laid out. I hate that big vase in the living room and that turquoise furniture."

That turquoise furniture was actually a muted powder blue game table and chairs—high-end furniture that had belonged to my grandparents. Okay, she could have seen all that through the windows.

"I've seen that glass shower your husband built and the special sink he put in the bathroom for you. I know you have a small bathroom in the garage where you come into the house."

She couldn't have seen those from outside. "So maybe you broke into my house."

"You think I stole from you? I didn't need to break in. He brought me over there when you were in Dayton taking care of your mother."

"My mother isn't in Dayton." I tried to sound casual, as if I were brushing her off. I knew it wasn't working, but I had to play it that way. My hands felt sticky and clammy, and my heart raced.

"Oh, I mean Toledo. I know every time you go to take care of her. Why do you think he tells you to spend the night and not drive back the same day?"

Bingo—I'd visited Mom last week. My stomach knotted. *Keep it cool, MJ; you have four coworkers just outside, and the office door is wide open.*

"So, why did you call me?"

"He told me he loved me; now he's f—ing my best friend. We have a baby together. I gave him what you couldn't give him."

Sucker punch. Didn't see that coming either.

"He's texting me right now. I'm going to get him on a three-way call so you can hear him, okay? Just don't say anything."

It wasn't okay with me, but I felt myself tumbling into this sudden flood of partial facts and unspoken threats. I hoped the flotsam and jetsam that swirled around me didn't come from the shipwreck of my forty-four-year marriage.

She put me on hold. The call disconnected. She called back. I picked up the phone and hit the mute button. I had no doubt the male voice on the other end was my husband's. I couldn't breathe.

"Kiana, what's wrong with you?" he asked.

"You're f—ing my best friend. You started when I was incarcerated." Here, I'm sure I rolled my eyes. "And you're f—ing your other tenants, too!"

"Kiana, you and I were done long before that."

"I have your wife on the line. Mary, you can hear this, can't you?"

Without a sound, I hung up.

How does one step back into the day-to-day routine after something like that? I stared at the phone, picked up a few papers from my desk, and watched them shake in my hands.

The phone rang again and displayed the same number. I let it ring through once but picked up when the caller persisted. Why? I'm not sure. A perverse need to know the truth? I was in too deep to ignore this now. How could my universe change so much in less than fifteen minutes?

She continued, "You don't believe me? I can tell you what his body looks like." Her language coarsened as she gave intimate details. "I can send you photos and videos of us, some from your house, some from mine. I know he likes to fall asleep in front of the TV after dinner and that you and he have cheese and crackers and apple slices on Sunday nights."

> *How could my universe change so much in less than fifteen minutes?*

Somehow, her account of our Sunday night ritual got to me even more than her description of my husband's body. I felt violated in every sense of the word, afraid I might vomit right there.

I tried to change the subject. "You mentioned being incarcerated."

It worked. "Yes, I was in jail, and your husband got me out. He told the judge he was my father." She paused and then added dramatically, "And I'm black."

I almost laughed at that. A little comic relief? The image of my once-blond-now-gray-haired-white-bearded husband passing himself off as this woman's father was funny even to me. That part of her story was too bizarre to believe.

"Give me your phone number or your email, and I'll send you pictures and videos. Or send me your address," she insisted.

"Surely you have my address."

"No. I could recognize your house if I drove past it, but I didn't pay any attention to the address when we went there."

"Too bad. You don't need any more information about me. What's your point?"

"Really, Mary? Are you that naive? Do you think I'm lying?"

"And what's your point in calling me?" I repeated.

She gave an exasperated huff and hung up.

I took a drink of water, decided I should shoot for an Academy Award, and went out into the main work area to see if my coworkers needed anything from me.

"Have you eaten yet?" one of them asked.

"No. I think maybe I'll take this afternoon off."

"Then go. We're fine. Get out of here."

But getting out wasn't quite that simple. I managed a department for a non-profit that employed persons with disabilities, and I couldn't just walk away from my job. It took another hour to fight a few fires, answer some emails that couldn't wait, and finally head for the door. I was still nauseated, and my throat was parched. I managed to swallow a few more sips of water as I stepped outside my office.

It was November 1, All Saints Day, a feast day in the Catholic Church. My husband and I had planned to attend Mass that evening at our parish. But I didn't think I could sit next to him in church now. Reaching for that Best Actress Award again, I called him.

"Hi, honey." I hoped I didn't sound too perky. I was aiming for just the right shade of vocal brightness. "I got out early and thought maybe I'd go to 5:30 Mass at St. Luke's tonight."

"That's great, hon. I actually got a later start than I'd planned this morning and ended up going at noon." He sounded normal and cheerful; nothing seemed amiss.

"Okay, see you when you get home." Typical conversation for us. Except nothing was typical anymore.

❖❖❖

I was dazed and in shock after my phone call with the "other woman." My life had turned upside down, and I needed to find a quiet place to sit, think, cry, and pray.

I drove to a local Catholic church, where I sat in the adoration chapel and tried to absorb what I'd learned. The earth had stopped spinning, leaving no sense of time, no to-do list, no fires to fight, no emails or voicemails to answer, no mundane tasks to demand my attention. This explosion had blown away all the trivia in my life.

Unable to think or pray, I felt as if I'd come to the bottom of a breath and could barely inhale again. I was too shocked for tears.

> *Unable to think or pray, I felt as if I'd come to the bottom of a breath and could barely inhale again.*

I sat motionless, my eyes closed, my shoulders slumped, my hands resting in my lap, my mind blank.

In the stillness, I pictured myself as a little child with God at my side. He took me by the right hand and began to lead me away. I looked over my shoulder at my husband, also a small child, and reached out my other hand to him. Then God said, "No, he can't come with us now. He'll come later, but not now."

That left me with a sense of peace and assurance that God would take care of both me and my husband, regardless of our circumstances. As I attended Mass, I was able to sing through the tears that streamed down my face and took that as a sign I'd somehow be okay.

I went home to prepare dinner before my husband (I'll call him Glen in this book) arrived. Chicken soup was the only food I thought my stomach could handle. When Glen came home, I told him I had something important to discuss and asked him to skip his usual before-dinner drink so we could both be alert and awake for that conversation. He shrugged and raised his eyebrows a bit but agreed. We proceeded with our usual Monday night routine and ate dinner, seated side by side on the sofa, while we watched *The Voice* on television.

As the show ended, he looked over and asked, "So what's this important thing we need to talk about?"

I turned to face him. "First of all, I know that being right is one of your highest values. But honesty is one of mine. I want you to be totally truthful with me, even if it hurts, okay?"

"Okay." He nodded in agreement.

Taking a deep breath, I began. "I received a series of disturbing phone calls at work today. Whether or not it's true, we have a very dangerous and serious situation on our hands. Who is Kiana?"

Glen stared straight ahead for a few seconds and didn't look at me.

"She's someone who rented from me, and I helped her try to get her kids back. Her mother has custody of her kids. She fell behind in her rent, and I let it go longer than I should have. She went to jail for a while on a shoplifting charge and asked if some friends could stay there to take care of her dog and the house. Well, that didn't work out. They were on drugs, didn't pay the rent, and trashed the place. I think she's on drugs too. And she's gay."

"Well, she says you're the father of one of her children."

He looked up in surprise. "I can promise you that's not true. She had all three kids before I met her. She used to tell me only two of the kids were hers, but her mother says they're all Kiana's."

I tried to process what I'd learned about this woman: *liar, drug-user, bisexual, criminal, doesn't have custody of her own children.*

"She says you brought her here. She knows all kinds of things about us," I said.

"Well, she's pretty good on the internet."

"No. She knows intimate details about us, about the house, things she couldn't know just by looking through the windows. She says she's having an affair with you."

He hesitated, then admitted they'd been involved sexually, and yes, he'd brought her to our house, but only to show it to her.

Invisible bombs crashed all around me.

Glen went on. "She stole some of my tools and pawned them, but I got them back. She moved out of state a while back, after she trashed the rental house. Then she started calling me about a month ago and leaving messages that she wanted to get back together. I just ignored her. She called and texted me today. She even tried to tell me you were on the line."

"I was on the three-way call. I heard you," I said.

He frowned and picked up his phone. "What time did she call you?"

He scrolled through his messages and call log, as if it were important what time I'd heard their conversation.

I noted he didn't apologize.

"She says you lied to get her out of jail—that you told the judge you were her father."

"Well, that part's true."

"Are you crazy? How could you do this to us? You brought her into our house—my house—my space. You told her intimate details about us. You violated our marriage."

I wasn't ranting. I wanted to know. Why?

He didn't respond. All the while, I waited for some sign of remorse, but he remained distant and emotionless. I wondered, *Who are you, and when did you get a lobotomy?*

I retreated to our bedroom, no longer able to stay in the same room with this man who was now a stranger. I needed time to sort all this out. The clock on the nightstand displayed 9:50 p.m. It had taken less time than a reality show episode for my entire world to fall apart. Tears didn't come right away. I locked the bedroom door and tried to process our conversation while I numbly went through the motions of my bedtime ritual.

> *All the while, I waited for some sign of remorse, but he remained distant and emotionless.*

But there would be no sleep. My numbness gave way to fury and humiliation the moment I realized the full significance of what he'd told me. My husband had been sexually active with a drug-using, bisexual woman who'd had multiple partners. That meant he'd potentially exposed me to every sexually transmitted disease out there. I was horrified.

I tried to pray, but I was far too angry. My head throbbed, but not with pain. The veins in my neck bulged, as if I were about to explode. I took an extra dose of my blood pressure medication.

Shortly after midnight, still unable to sleep, I locked myself in the spare bedroom and pounded out about ten pages on my laptop to document the day's events and conversations. I wrote as if it were a novel, to distance myself from this bizarre scenario that couldn't possibly be happening in real life. My frenzied typing provided two hours of catharsis, but my agitation demanded a more physical outlet.

At 3:00 a.m., I flipped on all the lights, yanked the vacuum cleaner out of the closet, and proceeded to clean the house. I could hear the television in the living room, but my noisy tirade elicited no response from Glen.

I returned to bed around 4:30, after I emailed my boss and my HR manager to say I wouldn't be at work that day.

Forty-five minutes later, unable to fall asleep, I made my way to the kitchen. Glen was brewing his coffee and offered to make a cup of tea for me, as he did every morning. I declined, then made one myself and sipped it in the dark while he went to take a shower. For much of our marriage, we'd showered together nearly every day, but I'd made up my mind that would never happen again.

Afterward, he stood in the doorway and said, "I'm sorry." Again, his voice held no emotion.

I responded, "Do you realize that only took you nine hours?"

He shrugged and walked away.

That evening—after I'd spent, without a doubt, the worst and most humiliating day of my life being tested for every STD possible and pouring out my heart to my parish priest—Glen walked into the house, laughing at something he'd heard on talk radio, and asked me if I knew a certain talk show host. At that moment, I realized he had no clue how devastating his betrayal was to me. He simply expected I'd get over it and life would go on as usual.

I wondered who this stranger was—this man whose emotions seemed to have switched off when I'd confronted him. I'd expected at least some sign of remorse, some explanation, some attempt to seek my forgiveness. But none came.

I couldn't put the pieces of our marriage back together alone.

No matter your circumstances then or now, you can't do it alone, either. God is ready and waiting for you to call.

Chapter 2

RECOGNIZING WHO DID WHAT TO WHOM

YOU'VE BEEN BETRAYED—if not by your spouse's infidelity, then by some other breach of your marriage vows to love and cherish each other until death. That betrayal is a fracture of the deepest level of your trust, and you probably find it hard to place your confidence in anyone—perhaps even God. You're not alone. That's a normal and natural reaction to the deep hurt you've experienced. You may think, *I did all the right things. I was a good wife and mother. I loved my husband and my children. We went to church every Sunday, read the Bible, prayed together. How could God let this happen to me?*

It's important to remember who did what to whom. God didn't betray you. The choices and actions of your human spouse, coupled with your own responses and choices, led to the breakup of your marriage. Free will, that two-edged sword, is a powerful and fearful weapon that can lead to glory or destruction. I don't mean to imply that you're responsible for your divorce. You may have fought for your marriage with all your might and prayed day and night for your spouse to change, and it seems your prayers were

> *You might even be angry with God for allowing this to happen or wonder what you did to make God punish you.*

in vain. You might even be angry with God for allowing this to happen or wonder what you did to make God punish you. Those are very human responses. God has heard them before, and He understands your anguish and frustration. Even Jesus wept tears and sweated blood.

Before you dismiss me as just another goody-goody Christian spouting platitudes, let me tell you that I do pray a lot—sort of an ongoing conversation—but sometimes those prayers have contained words like *a—hole* and *jerk*. I've suffered the profound grief, anger, and confusion common to most persons who experience divorce, and I want to share with honesty and transparency the lessons that have helped me along the way. Some of those lessons are profound; others are down to earth. I don't always walk this journey with enthusiasm or grace, but I'm gradually progressing toward a better, more whole version of myself. Through it all, I've learned that—regardless of how angry, hurt, lonely, hopeless, or betrayed I may feel—I can't travel this road without God at my side.

This is what I believe God has taught me, and what I must share with you: "You who are rejected, broken, unwanted—you are Mine. I love you. You are still beloved."

Chapter 3

SURVIVING THE UNTHINKABLE

YOUR WORLD HAS SHATTERED. Whether you were blindsided by your spouse's infidelity, as I was, or you reached your limit after years of abuse; whether you initiated the divorce or your spouse's decision to leave was thrust upon you—you find yourself at the edge of a cliff in the darkest of nights, unable to see anything ahead and unwilling or unable to return to the life you've known.

Even under normal circumstances, our lives are full of ups and downs, peaks and valleys. Writer and theologian C. S. Lewis called it the Law of Undulation. Saint Ignatius of Loyola saw it as cycles of consolation and desolation—events and periods of time when we're drawn closer to God or away from Him. Sometimes, those valleys are so deep they fall outside the normal realm of human experience, and we find ourselves cast so far into the pit of desolation it's difficult to imagine ever climbing out again. Surely the breakup of a marriage causes extreme desolation—a wounding of mind, body, soul, and spirit that threatens to destroy the very essence of your being.

Both Lewis and Ignatius advised, and modern psychologists agree, that a person in desolation should avoid major decisions. Unfortunately, divorce forces you to make many life-changing choices and decisions at a time when you're the least confident and most vulnerable.

Your life has turned upside down, and you can't avoid the questions that bombard you: Where will you live? What will you tell family and friends? How will you support yourself? How can you deal with your anger and hurt? Whom can you trust? And if you have children at home, the questions and decisions are even more urgent. You're in no shape to make those decisions alone.

> *Divorce forces you to make many life-changing choices and decisions at a time when you're the least confident and most vulnerable.*

Where do you start? First, I suggest you place God at the head of your team. You may not be happy with or trust His plan as it appears now, but to weather the storm of your divorce and emerge from it intact, you need the virtues and gifts that come through the Holy Spirit: wisdom, understanding, knowledge, courage, faith, hope, love, and a host of others. In short, you need all the help you can get, so why not go to the Source for that help?

There's an easy but effective way to bring moments of God's peace into your life. Though you may feel you're drowning in a torrent of events beyond your control, you can regain some sense of clarity and direction by taking a few minutes throughout your day to sit in silence, close your eyes, and breathe. You could practice this first thing in the morning when you wake up, before going to bed at night, or even for a few minutes while sitting in your car in the parking lot before or after work. This simple exercise of stillness in the midst of crisis allows you to process and assess the situation, helps you to remember God is in charge, and can prevent or minimize hasty, irrational actions you may later regret.

Don't force this exercise; view it as a respite, a way to give yourself small oases of peace in the midst of the chaos that surrounds you. This isn't yoga or New Age meditation. It's God's long-standing advice from Psalm 46, written in a time of war and trouble: "Be still and know that I am God."

Take this popular way of meditating on the verse and make it yours:
Be still and know that I am God.
Be still and know that I am.
Be still and know.
Be still.
Be.

Chapter 4

COPING WITH EMOTIONAL OVERLOAD

DIVORCE TURBOCHARGES your emotions and floods you with anger, rage, hurt, confusion, fear, anxiety, sadness, disappointment, frustration, guilt, and loneliness. Don't try to ignore or bury those feelings, even though they may be completely alien to you. They're real and powerful, and you don't need to be ashamed of them. However, you can't always express them, so how do you deal with that emotional overload? It's important to find safe, healthy ways to cope with negative emotions and stress now, so you can avoid or minimize serious damage to your mental and physical health in the future.

A few weeks after I filed for divorce, I shared my story with a coworker. The intensity of her response shocked me. She broke down and sobbed, "How could he do that to you? You don't deserve that! No one deserves to be treated that way!" Her face distorted in pain, and her body shook with emotion.

She told me her husband had left her for another woman ten years earlier, after he'd emptied their bank account and humiliated her. Eventually, she took him back, but she felt their relationship had never really healed. Now she suffered from chronic back pain, digestive disorders, severe weight gain, depression, and other maladies she attributed to holding her real feelings inside.

As I listened to her, I realized I could end up like this poor woman who erupted like a human volcano in front of me. Her story heightened my awareness of the damaging effects of suppressed negative emotions like anger, hurt, and grief. At that moment, I decided I wouldn't allow my divorce to destroy my health if I had any say in the matter.

Work out anger in a safe physical manner.

Two months into my divorce process, I ended up in bed with bronchitis for two weeks, unable to do much more than sleep most of the time. Despite medication and rest, I didn't improve. As I lay in bed and tried not to cough, it occurred to me that I was very angry and not able to express that anger because Glen and I still lived in the same house while we prepared to sell it. Maybe that pent-up anger was making me sick! But how could I get rid of it?

I pondered this dilemma and hatched a plan. Dressed in my robe and slippers, I headed for the garage and found a pair of safety glasses, a hammer, and a piece of lumber about thirty inches long. I carried all this into the basement, propped the board at an angle so it would break when I hit it, and began to pound on it with all my might. Every time the board broke, I repositioned it and hit it again. I continued until all that remained were splinters of wood strewn across the basement floor. I didn't clean up the mess. I wanted it to send a message, and

> **"** *Maybe that pent-up anger was making me sick!* **"**

besides, I might need to do this again. Bathed in sweat, I returned to bed and slept.

I awoke feeling much better and recovered fully within a couple days. I still view this as a healthy, empowering act that helped me break free of victimhood. When I shared this story with a married friend who'd never suffered the same level of betrayal, she frowned and suggested I might need some professional help with my anger. I laughed and replied, "Are you kidding? That was the best anger therapy I could ever experience!"

Take time to reboot.

Except for my bout with bronchitis, I took only one day off work for self-care during the initial months of my divorce. Sometimes it was therapeutic to go to work and forget about everything else, but I knew that type of denial was only a temporary fix. Eventually, I had to get away for some R & R. I wrote in my journal, *I desperately need to take some long walks on a beach somewhere.*

A few weeks later, my sister and her husband invited me to vacation with them in Emerald Isle, North Carolina, and I jumped at the opportunity. I spent an entire week near the ocean with people I love and enjoy. We ate good food, drank good wine, rented movies at night, slept in every morning, and laughed and talked. Best of all, I walked the beach alone for hours every day.

Instead of hunting for perfect shells, however, I found myself drawn to those that were broken and worn. I remembered a story I'd read about a woman who'd walked along a beach as she pondered her own losses and looked for solace amid major disruption to her life's plan. She'd picked up a scallop shell and initially discarded it because it was broken instead of whole. Then she felt called to examine it again, to discover its unique beauty. This shell, battered and broken by countless crashing ocean waves and storms, became for her a source of inspiration and hope, perhaps even a message of grace.

I started to look for shells that were damaged, and I realized that included most of the shells on the beach. I began to see the beautiful colors and designs in each of them, despite their injuries, and sometimes because of them. Each shell had been shaped by forces beyond its control, and each was beautiful in its own way. In fact, there would be no beach at all if it weren't for the tiny fragments of broken shells that make up the sand.

Predictable symmetry may be the ideal, but it's certainly not the only way nature expresses beauty and perfection. Why did I think my own life should be without brokenness? Why should I be one of the few "perfect" shells? I decided to make a conscious effort to find the good in my own situation, however fractured it might be.

> *Why did I think my own life should be without brokenness? Why should I be one of the few "perfect" shells?*

Yes, my marriage was over, but my life was not. Though it no longer conformed to my former image of perfection, perhaps I might discover the beauty in its new design.

At the end of the week, I went home rested and refreshed in body, mind, and spirit, better prepared to face the challenges that lay ahead.

Can't get to the beach? A trip to a local park, a stroll through a garden, or even a spin through the mall can help.

Chapter 5

BATTLING FEAR AND WORRY

AFRAID? OF COURSE YOU ARE—and for good reason. Divorce introduces a host of changes and uncertainty, and it's important to face them with realism and keep them in perspective. But when the foundation you've built your life upon crumbles, your perspective becomes skewed and distorted. It's easy for fear and worry to attack and threaten to overwhelm you.

Sometimes fear is defined as False Evidence Appearing Real. It often begins with a what-if question that snowballs out of control, a conclusion based upon a premise that isn't true or hasn't happened and may never occur.

Irrational fear never comes from God. It's a powerful tool in the hands of the enemy, who can use it to pry apart any chink in your armor. Since divorce shreds your armor, it makes you especially vulnerable to fear, anxiety, and worry.

I learned firsthand that fear is a spirit that can possess you when you allow it to take hold. That sounds like something out of *The Exorcist*, but bear with me while I explain.

Over the course of our divorce negotiations, Glen and I continued to live together in the same house for over four months. Glen's attorney had advised him not to leave or it could weaken his case, and, initially, I clung to the fantasy that I could keep the house. When it became obvious that wasn't practical, I continued to live there as we prepared to sell it. It was awkward and strange, I think, for both of us.

> *I learned firsthand that fear is a spirit that can possess you when you allow it to take hold.*

During that time, Glen offered me several different financial settlement proposals—some delivered through his attorney, others presented directly by him. Most of them split our assets based on the ratio of his lifetime earnings or his Social Security contributions to mine. Needless to say, he always came out ahead.

Eventually, I was worn down, heartsick, and exhausted. I just wanted this ordeal to be over so I could move on. When Glen handed me yet another agreement weighted in his favor, I decided to give up and told him I'd accept it. I emailed my attorney and stated I was ready to sign the settlement attached to my message. He summoned me right away to his office and showed me in black and white what that agreement meant in terms of my financial future.

"You'll have to work the rest of your life," he pointed out. "And your husband will laugh all the way to the bank."

At first, I didn't change my mind. I didn't care who won. This wasn't a game, and there'd be no winners. Then he caught my attention.

"Mary Jo, this is a terrible settlement. If you insist on signing it, I'll do something I've done only once in my twenty-seven years of practice."

"What's that?" I asked.

"I'll fire you as a client." His eyes told me he wasn't kidding. "The law says you're entitled to half. Let's get this done with the justice you deserve."

He produced a document he'd prepared that divided our assets evenly and provided a more secure financial future for me. I signed it for submission to the court, and I knew Glen wouldn't be happy.

All the way home, my thoughts swirled. The more I thought about what I'd done, the more fearful I became. I imagined how angry Glen would be. He'd never been violent or abusive, but did I really know him? I hadn't thought he'd be unfaithful, but I was wrong about that. I didn't know this man after all, did I? And he carried a gun. Not only that, but he had other guns in the house. How many times had I heard about murders and murder-suicides that involved divorce? Sweat prickled under my arms, and my mouth was so dry I could barely swallow. I tossed and turned all night.

The next morning, my anxiety continued as I sat through a meeting at work. As it ended, I asked the rest of the staff to stay.

"By now, you all know I'm going through a divorce," I began. My voice trembled. I took a deep breath. "I'm not sure how my husband's going to react to something I did yesterday, and I want you to be prepared in case he shows up here and things get out of hand."

I proceeded to lay out an emergency plan that directed everyone in the front offices to evacuate into the factory area. I cautioned my coworkers not to try to rescue me in the event of this plan's mobilization and pointed out that our "No Firearms" sign in the lobby wouldn't deter Glen from bringing a gun into the building.

Their eyes widened as I went on. I don't unhinge easily, and they could see I was very serious.

"Can't you get a restraining order?" one of them asked.

"No. I have no reason to ask for one at this point. He's

never done anything to threaten me." I'm sure my answer didn't comfort her any more than it did me.

For the rest of the day, my stomach churned, my head buzzed, and I was damp with sweat, though I shivered and couldn't get warm. By the end of the day, I was so terror-stricken, I knew how fear felt and tasted and smelled.

When I arrived home, Glen's truck was in the driveway. That big diesel Silverado with the loud muffler had become a symbol of all the power I imagined he held over me. I was so terrified, I couldn't get out of my car for several minutes. Finally, I breathed a prayer for courage and protection and went into the house.

Glen was fixing his dinner and greeted me as if nothing out of the ordinary had happened. I stood in the kitchen and tried to determine if he was putting on an act. Then I realized there was no way he could have known anything about the new settlement my attorney had drawn up. It probably hadn't even gone to the court yet. There certainly hadn't been enough time for his lawyer to pass it on to him.

I'd spent over twenty-four hours controlled by fear—a fear I generated myself and fed in my mind until it overwhelmed and possessed me. Was there reason to be concerned? Yes. But I'd allowed my concern to grow into a terror so big it left no room for rational thought or behavior.

I remembered the Scripture verse, "For God did not give us a spirit of cowardice, but rather of power and love and self-control" (2 Timothy 1:7). My fear made me forget the power and grace available to me. I was so anxious, I forgot to bring my concerns to God, to ask the Holy Spirit for wisdom and the ability to see clearly. When I felt myself becoming fearful, I should

> *My fear made me forget the power and grace available to me.*

have asked God to give me a perspective based on truth, not a distortion of the facts. Instead, I wasted an entire day of my life as I cowered and bowed to my fear. In effect, I turned it into a god. Maybe now you understand what I mean when I say fear is a spirit, and it doesn't come from God. God is Perfect Love, and "perfect love drives out fear" (1 John 4:18).

Ask God to show you His truth.

Worry is fear's little brother. At first, it doesn't look very threatening. While fear seems to loom bigger and bigger from some external cause, worry often starts out as a legitimate concern that worms its way into our thoughts until it, too, grows big enough to take over and distort our thinking.

By nature, I'm not a worrier. Much of the time, I'd prefer to fly by the seat of my pants and take each day as it comes rather than think very far ahead and worry about things that might never happen. But there are circumstances that do require significant attention and consideration for the future. Because divorce changes nearly every aspect of life, it creates the opportunity for reasonable and justifiable concerns to develop into persistent worries and anxieties that make it difficult to see situations with clarity and make decisions based on truth.

> *Worry is fear's little brother. At first, it doesn't look very threatening.*

My mother is an artist, and she taught me to "see what's really there"—the lights and darks, the positive and negative shapes, the mix of colors that make up highlights and shadows. This is an essential skill every visual artist must develop to overcome a false picture produced by the mind.

Almost everyone experiences a phenomenon called *schemata*, which occurs because the human brain produces a symbol or mental picture for nearly every word or concept in one's vocabulary.[1] Ask someone to draw a picture of a tree, and he'll likely produce a straight brown trunk topped by a ruffled green circle. Detail-oriented persons may color round red apples on their trees, but, in reality, most trees look far different from the symbol in the mind's eye. Ask for a drawing of an eye, and you'll probably get a fairly symmetrical almond shape with a full circle in the center and a dark dot for a pupil. This common symbol hardly resembles a real human eye, but it's a nearly universal graphic response.

My favorite example of schemata occurred in a drawing class when we students were asked to sketch the profile—or side view—of our instructor's face. The woman next to me faithfully followed the outline of the forehead, the nose, the lips, and the chin and produced a passable likeness of the model's profile. Then she proceeded to draw two almond-shaped eyes on the side of this head because her brain told her the human face has two eyes!

> *What our brains tell us isn't always the way things are. What do we miss when we don't "see what's really there?"*

What our brains tell us isn't always the way things are. What do we miss when we don't "see what's really there"? When worries, anxieties, and fears overload our minds, we find it difficult to sort out what's really happening around us. We human beings are body, mind, and spirit, but we often forget to use our spiritual senses to discern truth.

We can break the cycle of worry by asking the Holy Spirit for enlightenment, the ability to see God's truth and reality instead of the distorted picture we hold in our minds. It

---

[1] Frank Covino, *Controlled Painting* (Westport, Connecticut: North Light Publishers, 1982), 49.

requires a conscious effort to pause and breathe, to quiet the frantic voices that cry out for our attention. Only then can we open our minds to the peace God wants to give us, the peace that allows us to listen and hear His voice, to seek His truth and see our situation as He wants us to see it.

When our house sold, I took a short-term lease on an apartment, but I was sure I wanted another house with a beautiful yard, a garden, flowers, and trees—although, to tell the truth, I'd never been one to enjoy yardwork. My son asked me to think in terms of lifestyle and suggested I look into condos. He showed me a community where one of his friends lived on a small lake that had once been a quarry. It was lovely, but there was nothing available in my price range, and I continued to fret over where I'd live. My concern became almost obsessive, as I combed the internet each day to look for a suitable house.

One morning, my mother called and said, "I think your father's trying to get a message to you." My father had died fifteen months earlier, and my mother is the least "spooky" person I know, so I paid attention to what she was saying.

"I woke up this morning with the song 'Whispering Hope' playing in my head, and I can't get it to stop. That's the first song I ever heard your dad sing, and I want you to listen to the words."

Then she sang it to me. In the song, I heard my father tell me to be patient and wait, that God would take care of me. It gave me great peace. I told the Lord I'd stay in the apartment as long as He wanted, and I stopped house hunting.

Two weeks later, my daughter-in-law called to tell me a condo in that complex on the lake had just come on the market. She had no idea why it had shown up in her Facebook feed, and neither did I, but I was thrilled! I called my realtor right away, scheduled a walk-through, and toured it with my son that afternoon. It had been a casual bachelor pad for two brothers and needed to be updated, but it had good bones and lots of potential. Besides, I liked to renovate houses and had a long history of remodeling projects under my belt. It would be good therapy. I submitted an offer within my budget, and the seller accepted it.

Even if you can't afford much, the Lord will nonetheless help you find a place you can make your own. A place where you can be safe, comfortable, and able to breathe again.

Chapter 6

GRIEVING MANY LOSSES

I STOOD IN THE STATIONERY AISLE and scanned the racks for a bridal shower card, when a section marker caught my eye: *Divorce*. Really? I couldn't resist. I had to see what greetings one might send for the occasion. What I found made me cringe. Out of about a dozen cards, I saw only one that treated the subject with even a shade of respect and sensitivity. Many were quite creative; most were suggestive, if not downright lewd. There was enough dark humor in those cards to fuel a whole evening of stand-up comedy, and had I not been in the middle of my own divorce, I would have laughed out loud at some of them. I won't say I never engaged in that form of bitter and sarcastic humor, especially early in my divorce process, but it always felt hollow and empty.

The end of married life is a death that merits grief on many levels. Although jokes, witty cards, and divorce parties may offer humorous, short-term support, they're only superficial (and often disrespectful and childish) efforts to deflect and ignore this very deep and real pain. As with any grief, you must face it, acknowledge it, and resolve it, or it will, at some point, rear its head and demand your attention.

> **The end of married life is a death that merits grief on many levels.**

It's difficult to tally the many losses associated with the breakup of a long-term marriage. Some are obvious, and some are much more subtle. Your own list might include loss of love, companionship, trust, identity, self-esteem, sense of wholeness and well-being, dreams and hopes for the future, personal life direction, roles and relationships among family and friends, status in society, financial security, home, and neighborhood. The losses are overwhelming.

Each of these losses is accompanied by grief, a normal and natural reaction, complex and unique to each person. The Grief Recovery Institute defines grief as "the conflicting feelings caused by the end of or change in a familiar pattern of behavior."[2] In this definition, you can see that even if your divorce is a welcome relief from years of abuse, you'll still experience significant grief when you leave your marriage.

Acknowledge the end of the life you shared with your spouse.

Your divorce has dealt you a crushing blow, especially if you had no idea it was coming. The shock can paralyze you. Like me, you may waver between bitter anger and hopeless despair, unable to think clearly and unsure of what you really want.

When I first learned of my husband's infidelity, I was so upset I went nearly thirty-eight hours without sleep. That, coupled with the emotional shock, threw me into a twilight zone where nothing seemed real. Externally, I went

---

[2] John W. James and Russell Friedman, *The Grief Recovery Handbook (20th Anniversary Expanded Edition)* (New York: Harper-Collins Publishers, 2009), 3.

through the motions at home and at work; internally, I felt as if some vital part of me had died. Even simple tasks overwhelmed me. I had trouble remembering names and faces. I forgot words during simple conversation. I missed appointments unless they were written down and right in front of me.

> *You may waver between bitter anger and hopeless despair, unable to think clearly and unsure of what you really want.*

Just slogging through each day was all I could manage. I certainly didn't have the energy or mental clarity to look very far ahead.

Though I knew I couldn't remain with Glen, I don't think I allowed myself to fully grasp that our life together was over. Civil divorce isn't the answer for everyone, but I was compelled to file for my safety and sanity. We were intimate right up to the time I learned he'd been unfaithful, and his sexual association with someone who used drugs and had multiple partners threatened my health and possibly even my life. How many more adulterous encounters had there been, or would there be? I couldn't continue to expose myself to this. Glen had absolutely no regret, and there was no hope for reconciliation.

While we lived together for those months and prepared to sell the house, it's not surprising there were times I slipped into our old routine. I came home from work and fixed dinner. Since I was cooking for myself, I figured I might as well make enough for him. There were evenings we both sat in the living room and watched the same television program. Sometimes, I could almost forget.

One night, I had a dream in which Glen and I worked on a remodeling project, something we'd done well together many times during our marriage. I held a ladder as he hung a light fixture. In my dream, I looked up at him and said to myself, *See? This isn't so bad. We can work it out.* Then—still in my dream—I remembered the reason for our divorce and said out loud, "Oh, no, we can't!"

I woke up and faced head-on the truth I'd feared: my life with Glen was over. I had to leave it behind.

Know that God journeys with you and shares your pain.

I'd hired a company to move me into my apartment, and the real estate agent was on his way to our house with the final seller paperwork for both of us to sign. As I packed amid boxes and bins, Glen handed me the latest in a series of financial settlement agreements he'd drawn up to counter the one my attorney submitted. I told him I'd read it after I finished packing, but he insisted. I glanced at the pages, set it aside, and continued to box up my belongings.

The realtor arrived, and the three of us sat around the kitchen table. He passed the papers for my signature. I signed and handed them to Glen, who slid them back to the realtor.

"I'll sign these when she signs what I gave her." He sat back and smiled, his arms crossed. Checkmate.

I was furious. We had a full-price offer and an agent who'd bent over backwards to complete this sale. My spine stiffened, and the blood rushed to my face. "I will not be blackmailed," I responded. My tone was icy and controlled. I wielded each word like a weapon.

The realtor rose and excused himself after he'd made it clear he wouldn't go out of his way to show our house again if we impeded this sale. I waited until he left. Then I screamed all my anger and frustration at my husband, who calmly walked out the door and drove away.

I sank down under the full weight of the past five months. How could this happen? This man I'd loved had positioned himself as my enemy. I hadn't asked for or declared war, and yet we'd just drawn clear battle lines. In many ways, I was still in shock and holding fast to the illusion that—at some level—Glen *must* still care about me! Now, that illusion shattered.

Shaking with anger, I called my attorney and told him what had happened. He assured me he'd try to contact Glen's lawyer, who was out of the country at the time. When I hung up, my mind raced through worst-case scenarios. What if Glen wouldn't sign and we couldn't sell the house? I could sue him for the money that should have been mine, but that could take months. What if we both stopped paying the mortgage and the bank foreclosed on the house? What if? What if?

Alone in my kitchen, I cried out to God that I needed a just judge, someone to take my side and fight for me. I'd done everything I could to fend for myself, but my own efforts weren't enough to protect me from this injustice.

"Lord, Your word says You hear the cry of the poor. I need You to take care of this!" My head and shoulders sagged as I put it in God's hands and surrendered the outcome. I could do nothing more.

> *I'd done everything I could to fend for myself, but my own efforts weren't enough to protect me from this injustice.*

Early the next morning, my attorney called to tell me Glen had signed the required papers. I don't know what his lawyer said to him, but it worked. The sale of the house went through without further complications, and there were no more unjust settlement proposals. I know God came to my aid to make it happen.

We received our final divorce decree and closed the sale of our house the same week that marked the fiftieth anniversary of our first date. Closing, by the way, took place at 3:00 p.m. on Good Friday, the Hour of Mercy, which gave new meaning to the words "It is finished."

I'd moved into my apartment two weeks earlier. We met at my attorney's office to sign the check from the sale of the house. I handed Glen his birth certificate, Social Security card, college diploma, and other items I'd kept safe over the years. Our conversation was so civil and natural that my lawyer commended us on our continued ability to communicate. It felt surreal.

When we stepped outside, I noticed Glen had driven a different vehicle.

"Did you buy a new car?" I asked.

"No, the truck and the Jetta wagon are both in the shop, and this is a loaner," he responded. "The Jetta has so many miles, I'll probably have to replace it soon, though."

"Yeah, I should probably look for a newer car later in the year, too," I observed.

He paused a few seconds and then said, "Well, good luck."

"Yeah, you too." I was still talking about cars.

I got into my vehicle and drove two blocks before it hit me: *Oh my gosh! That's how we just ended a fifty-year relationship!*

Back at my office, I broke down and shared my sad story with a sympathetic coworker, and we cried together through lunchtime.

I still wish I had better closure. I'd wanted to sit across a table and tell Glen I hoped he'd get his act together and become the man God created him to be—or give some other equally self-satisfying speech—but instead, the flame of our fifty-year love fizzled out without even a puff of smoke.

For You

Grief will come in waves—maybe for years—and often when you least expect it. Just as your relationship with your spouse was one of a kind, so too, your grief is unique to you. It's never too early or too late to begin your journey toward recovery.

Chapter 7

Making Healthy Choices

I LOVE SWEETS, particularly chocolate, and food is usually the first thing I reach for when I'm stressed out. I also enjoy an occasional beer or glass of wine. In my emotional turmoil, I was tempted to reach for a drink or a bowl of ice cream—anything to comfort me and take the edge off my pain.

However, I realized the breakup of my marriage was a greater trauma than I'd ever experienced, and it wouldn't be over for a long time. That realization forced me to recognize the fragility of my overall health. Less than two years earlier, we'd moved both my ailing parents into our house for six months and then into a nursing home. My father died six months later. That year put a significant strain on my physical and mental health. It took months to get my blood pressure back under control, and I still occasionally broke out in hives. I knew I needed to take the stress of my divorce seriously or I'd be in big trouble. Short-term feel-good fixes—while sometimes very necessary—could also create long-term problems that would only make my situation worse.

With those concerns in mind, I decided to pay attention to what I fed my body, to make sure I ate healthy meals and limited my sweets. I made it a point not to drink alcohol during this time except for an occasional glass of wine with family or friends. My brain was foggy enough without adding alcohol to the mix, and I certainly didn't need its depressant effects.

Exercise regularly, get adequate rest, take good care of your general health.

The severe stress caused by the breakup of your marriage puts your overall health in danger. Sustained elevated levels of the stress-induced hormones adrenaline and cortisol—the body's fight-or-flight response—can put you at risk for high blood pressure, heart disease, lowered immune response, digestive disorders, headaches, and a long list of other health-threatening conditions. Divorce steals plenty from you. Don't let it rob you of your health, too!

❖❖❖

A few weeks into my own journey, I lost my senses of smell and taste. Visual migraines caused me to lose much of the vision in both eyes for about thirty minutes at a time, sometimes multiple times a day. My sleep was erratic, interrupted by vivid, wild dreams that left me exhausted. I also seemed to lose my sense of position in space, physically as well as metaphorically. One week, I broke my big toe on the open dishwasher door, and a few days later, I sliced open the back of my hand when I reached into a closet.

> *The severe stress caused by the breakup of your marriage puts your overall health in danger.*

A friend in healthcare cautioned that high cortisol levels could cause my symptoms. She advised me that rest and physical exercise could lower those levels. Normally, I'm not a big fan of exercise. In fact, I'm a bit of a slug, but my physical symptoms scared me, and I knew I had to do something to relieve them.

I found a small, family-owned gym that catered to the over-fifty crowd—where my cellulite and spider veins didn't look too out of place—and signed up to meet weekly with a trainer. I knew I needed the accountability to make me stick to a program that would net the results I wanted. Besides, it had been years since I'd set foot in a gym, and I had no idea how to use the equipment without risking injury or looking like an absolute fool.

At my first session, I was upfront with Mark, my trainer. "Look, I haven't been to a gym in over thirty years, and I don't want to hurt after every time I train with you or I'll probably quit coming."

His smile made me think I wasn't the first client who'd said that to him. "I think we can figure out some routines that'll work for you. Let's start with the rowing machine to get a baseline."

Ninety seconds on the rower, and I'd had enough. My legs felt like rubber as I walked to the elliptical, my next stop on the circuit. *Note to self,* I thought, lightheaded after only a minute on that machine, *I've got to eat more for lunch if I'm going to do this after work.*

Mark continued my assessment. "Well, your muscle tone's pretty good. You've got great flexibility, and your upper body strength is better than I expected. We need to work on your stamina and endurance."

Good. I wasn't a total wimp.

Regular workouts began to pay off. Over the next few months, my sleep improved, the visual migraines tapered off and eventually stopped, and my senses of taste and smell returned to normal. My sense of wellness and wholeness began to return. I started to feel more like myself. I even changed my mindset from "I *have to* go to the gym today" to "I *get to* go to the gym today." That, in itself, was a minor miracle.

Your body is as much a part of you as your mind, heart, and soul. It's not just a shell. It will be raised and glorified for all eternity. Even if you haven't been to the gym in years, take that first step. Any step.

Chapter 8

DEALING WITH FAMILY AND FRIENDS

OBVIOUSLY, DIVORCE AFFECTS your entire family. Your children—if you have them—will grieve, regardless of their ages. That subject deserves more attention than I'm prepared to give it in this book. If you have children living at home, I highly recommend you seek out age-appropriate material from a reliable source that's consistent with Church teaching. For example, many Catholic dioceses have Family Life offices that offer resources like support groups for parents and children, therapist referrals, and more.

Both my children were in their thirties at the time of the divorce. My conversation with each of them included a variation of the following:

"Your dad's always been a good father, and I don't want to destroy your relationship with him. You'll have to work that out yourselves. I don't want to make you choose sides or feel disloyal to either one of us. We both love you."

My son was very open with me and soon set his own boundaries: "Mom, you know I'm here for you and I'll help you any way I can, but I can't be the sounding board for either your or Dad's anger. It's hard enough for me to deal with my own emotions."

Fair enough. I could honor his request.

I knew my daughter would be harder to read. She lives on the West Coast, and I didn't want to break the news to her over the phone. I waited until she had some time off so I could fly out to tell her in person. My visit would take place four weeks after I'd learned about Glen's betrayal.

The morning of my flight, Glen sat down in the living room and said, "We need to talk."

I stood, unsure what to expect. "Okay, what about?"

He continued, "I need to tell you where my head was."

I bit my tongue. I was pretty sure I knew exactly what part of his anatomy that involved.

He proceeded to tell me how much I'd changed over the past fifteen years or so, although he couldn't give me any particulars.

"Everybody changes," I shot back. "You've changed too."

I thought of all the changes we'd both experienced during that time: the deaths of both his parents, his being downsized into early retirement, his two back-to-back rotator cuff surgeries, three relocations, renovating a house, caring for my parents, and my father's dementia and death. We'd started a business, lost money during the Great Recession, and sold the business to the non-profit where I now worked. During that same period, our daughter had moved away, and our son had married.

Yes, we'd both experienced many changes. I thought we'd weathered those well, though, all things considered. It seemed odd he'd never said anything like that before.

"You didn't contribute enough to our retirement," he added.

The money thing again? Are you serious? You're using that *to justify adultery and betrayal?*

It was true. My Social Security income would be much less than his, but that's the case for many women my age who chose to stay home with their pre-school children before they entered or re-entered the workforce. That was a flimsy and pathetic excuse.

I held my hands out in front of me like a balance. "Retirement income or marriage vows? That doesn't make sense."

"I gave up on my marriage vows a long time ago," he said.

"How long ago?" I demanded.

"You don't want to know."

"You're right. I don't," I decided.

With that, he walked out and left me to ponder this latest absurdity.

Dumbfounded, I chose to put our conversation behind me and concentrated instead on the one I'd soon have with our daughter.

My first night with her, I broached the subject as we sat on her living room sofa.

"Has your brother told you what's going on?"

She picked up a newspaper and began to cut out coupons.

"No," she said. "He's a big boy now. He didn't need to send you all this way to tell me about his problems."

Oh boy, I thought. *She thinks his marriage is in trouble. Let me try this again.*

"Actually, this isn't about your brother. It's about your dad and me."

She continued her task without looking up.

"About a month ago, I got a phone call at work from one of his tenants who said she was having an affair with him. It turned out to be true, and he hasn't shown any signs of remorse or apology." I took a deep breath. "I can't stay with him. I've filed for divorce."

As I groped for more words, she continued to clip coupons. I thought she was trying to block me out.

I went on. "This isn't a grand love affair with somebody he even cares about. She's a drug user, has three kids who live with her mother, couldn't pay her rent, and went to jail for shoplifting. She called me because she's mad he's messing around with her best friend."

Then I added, "The only reason he gave me for his infidelity was that I hadn't contributed enough money to our retirement."

Finally, my daughter put the scissors down and looked at me. "That only works if he's trading up," she said.

I stared at her with my mouth open. Then I laughed. "What a perfect response! Oh, how I wish I'd said that to him!"

In the years since the divorce, both of our children have worked through the awkwardness of reshaping their relationship with their dad, and for that I'm thankful.

Communicate your needs and set boundaries as necessary.

I'm the oldest of four children, and I first dated Glen when I was fifteen, so he was a big brother to my siblings for a long time. Both of my sisters and my brother were stunned at the news of our impending divorce, and they were very angry at Glen. Similarly, my best friend, who'd known him since high school, was furious. They formed a close-knit support system for me, and initially I found it very helpful. However, their anger started to hurt when a couple of them voiced prior suspicions and speculations I didn't want to hear. I mentioned it to my son, and he threatened to stay home from the big family Christmas celebration if everyone would be talking about his dad.

I sent my family a group text: "I want to request a favor from all of you. We're all having a hard time processing this. Glen has been a very good father and also a very good son-in-law. Everyone's emotions are raw and run the whole gamut just as if he'd died, but our tendency is to vilify rather than sanctify him. My son doesn't want 'dad bashing,' even from me. He still has to maintain a relationship with his father, as difficult as that is and will be. If he thinks everyone's talking about this and making judgments, as we are, he'll choose to stay away from family gatherings. None of us wants that. My request is that, as a family, we take the high road on this. It doesn't mean I won't vent to you. Sometimes I need that, and I definitely need your support. Just avoid speculation, and don't voice your prior suspicions, because, frankly, that's not helpful. Please continue to pray for us and especially for Glen. I think that's our call. Thank you. I love you all. MJ"

I didn't need to say anything more.

Break the news in your own way.

You and your spouse didn't live in a vacuum. Your relationship extends outward into your circles of family, friends, neighbors, and even coworkers and business associates. Although you're not directly responsible for them and their reactions, they, too, will be affected by the breakup of your marriage.

Don't feel compelled to broadcast the news of your divorce to everyone. Although you may be active on social media, you should be discreet about using it as a platform to announce your divorce. You may be tempted to vent your anger and frustration via Facebook or Twitter, but your rants may come back to haunt you, as nothing you post online ever really goes away.

> *You may be tempted to vent your anger and frustration via Facebook or Twitter, but your rants may come back to haunt you.*

With the pending publication of this book and my involvement in divorce ministry, I faced the need to disclose our divorce to friends and extended family I hadn't yet told. We'd lived in several communities during our marriage and developed close relationships in each location, the kinds of friendships that allow you to go years without seeing each other and then pick up right where you left off.

I didn't want to tell them, not only because I knew they'd ache for us, but also because it meant I once more had to peel off the paper-thin skin that covered the wound I'd tried so hard to heal. When two different people from our past found me on Facebook and asked about my husband and family, I put off my response, unsure how to break the news.

Then I received an unexpected phone call from a dear friend who just wanted to catch up. As I'd predicted, my news shocked and saddened her, but instead of increasing my pain, our conversation contributed to my healing. I no longer felt I had to hide something shameful. She accepted me and mourned the loss of Glen as part of our foursome, while we remembered some of the crazy, fun times we'd shared since college days.

I decided to compose a general letter I could customize for each recipient. It spared me the trauma of recounting my story numerous times and gave me some control over how and what I wanted to disclose. It also lessened the possibility I'd be blindsided by chance encounters and phone calls that might prove awkward and uncomfortable.

❖❖❖

A few months after my divorce, my high school class met for an informal reunion. Although Glen and I had gone to different high schools, he'd attended the same church and grade school as many of my classmates. We'd been a couple since we were fifteen years old, so my friends knew him well. I hadn't yet told any of them about our divorce. The reunion would be my "coming out" party. I really didn't want to go. The thought of all those inevitable questions exhausted me.

Just as I feared, when I walked in alone, several people came up and asked about Glen. I fumbled through a few awkward answers before I saw some of my old crowd. They waved me to their table, where I sat down and shared the news. One friend, divorced many years ago, gave a humorous one-liner to anyone who came up to talk with me to spare me the pain of having to tell my story multiple times. The next day, she texted me: "I'm so glad you came. I'm sure it wasn't easy, but you've never been afraid of a challenge. You've got this."

Those three words—*you've got this*—were like a gentle rain that watered my crushed spirit and awakened my dormant self-confidence. I realized other people believed in me because they knew who I was apart from my marriage. It gave me hope I could rediscover that person.

Divorce does not define you. "You" are still there!

Chapter 9

RELIEVING SPIRITUAL AND CREATIVE DRYNESS

I'VE ALWAYS LOVED MUSIC, but I don't let the radio blare just for the noise. I appreciate some quiet downtime, especially after work. However, coming home to the silence of a house that echoed with my sadness was almost unbearable. I needed to fill that void with something to lift my spirits and nurture my soul.

A good deal of scientific research supports the effectiveness of music as a valid therapy to treat anxiety, depression, mental and physical pain, and other disorders. That should come as no surprise. God Himself is goodness, truth, and beauty. Through music and the beauty of the created world, He brings hope and His healing touch.

The most effective music selections to ease anxiety and aid relaxation are fairly slow and flowing, around sixty beats per minute, and are primarily instrumental rather than songs with lyrics—not head-banging party pieces with a strong, fast beat.

A shopping experience years ago at the Nature Company showed me how effective music therapy can

> *The most effective music selections to ease anxiety and aid relaxation are fairly slow and flowing, around sixty beats per minute, and are primarily instrumental.*

be. As I meandered through the store, I felt a sense of wholeness and enhanced well-being. It was so obvious, I stopped to analyze my surroundings to see if I could discover the cause of that feeling. The entire environment of the store provided customers with an experience of sensory beauty. A water feature bubbled at the entrance; the lighting was warm and intimate; the aroma of complimentary herbal tea filled the air. But what affected me most was the music that played in the background—a piano instrumental that incorporated natural sounds like ocean waves, rain, sea birds, and whale songs. I felt almost physically lifted by this music. Needless to say, I bought the album, *San Juan Suite* by Michael Gettel. It never failed to raise my spirits, and my family enjoyed it as much as I did.

During my divorce, with that in mind, I thought about the kinds of music I liked, pieces to lift my mood without being too jarring. I developed my own Pandora playlists: easy listening piano and instrumental, Yo-Yo Ma on cello, Michael W. Smith, light classical piano, guitar instrumental, Andrea Bocelli, Sarah Brightman. Soon I had multiple selections to suit my mood. They became my drug of choice to soothe away self-pity and negative thoughts.

One piece showed up from time to time on several playlists and became my favorite, although I wasn't familiar with it. When I finally looked at my iPad during the song, I laughed out loud at the title: "Time to Say Goodbye." God does work in mysterious ways!

Get in touch with nature.

As a short-term housing solution, I moved from our lovely ranch home on a heavily wooded lot into a second-story unit in a large apartment complex. Since I worked in a windowless office every day, I soon felt sterile and claustrophobic. Nothing around me seemed to draw my attention away from my own troubles. Spring gave way to summer, and I craved the sights, sounds, and scents of the forest that had surrounded my house. I knew I had to seek them out, if only for a few moments at a time.

My apartment was near a neighborhood with beautiful houses, trees, hills, and sidewalks. I decided to take a daily walk there after work. Early every evening, I set out to explore the neighborhood and enjoy the different kinds of trees, flowers, and plants I saw along the way. I made it a point to look for beauty and joy in the sights and sounds around me. Sometimes I offered short prayers of gratitude for simple pleasures like the antics of a squirrel or the songs of cardinals or the tap-tapping of a woodpecker. The breeze in my hair, the sun on my face, the play of light through the leaves overhead, the scent of a rose garden—I began to notice the beauty in my everyday surroundings and to view each glimpse of joy as a gift. I felt myself reawakening. I came to view my daily walks as an effective part of my healing process.

> *I came to view my daily walks as an effective part of my healing process.*

My efforts to connect with nature soon yielded other benefits. I found I couldn't indulge in self-pity or imaginary conversations while I tried to enjoy the scenic beauty around me. My mood improved significantly. I had more energy, slept better, and came to view my daily walks as an effective part of my healing process.

About that time, my church formed a group of runners and walkers to participate in a half marathon for charity. There were several months of training before the event, with group runs and walks scheduled every Saturday morning. Though I didn't want to run, I enjoyed walking, so I signed up.

The weekly training events proved to be just the right amount of social contact. We started with group exercise and motivational cheers and then headed out along the Monon Trail, a popular paved Rails-to-Trails path near where I live in Indianapolis. I could stay with a group or walk at my own pace. Participants were friendly but also comfortable with those who preferred to train alone. The trail was so beautiful and invigorating—physically, mentally, and spiritually—that I didn't mind getting up at 6:00 a.m. every Saturday to train.

The Indianapolis Monumental Marathon/Half Marathon/5K took place the first Saturday in November. My sister Beth, who'd trained separately, joined me for the race. We drove downtown to meet our group hours before dawn in near-freezing weather, but we were pumped. It was Beth's birthday, and her "Birthday Girl" bib drew greetings from participants and spectators alike. The pre-race atmosphere vibrated with anticipation as over fifteen thousand racers gathered in their designated corrals. We shivered in the midst of nearly eight thousand half marathoners as we tried to keep our feet and hands warm and took photos before the race began.

We started out strong, but within the first two miles, I developed a sharp pain along the top of my right foot and had to stop several times to adjust my shoe. That hadn't happened in all my months of training, and I thought it was because I'd let my feet get too cold before the race. I later realized I'd unconsciously tried to match strides with Beth, who's several inches taller, which threw off my whole gait. Despite that, we immersed ourselves in the spirit of the race. We sang with the sidewalk musicians along the way, laughed at the cheers of the partying spectators who toasted us from their porches, and encouraged other racers along the course. As we passed by my son's volunteer station, he ran out to take our pictures and walk a few blocks with us.

A half marathon is 13.1 miles. That's a long way to walk. The first five or six miles were fun. We laughed and talked as sisters do. The next five miles or so wound through neighborhoods that didn't celebrate the event—or perhaps they'd all gone inside by the time we came through. The atmosphere was much quieter as participants buckled down, determined to go the distance. By the time we reached the final three-mile stretch, the temperature was in the low forties, and a light mist covered my glasses. I wished I'd brought a visor or ball cap to keep them dry. Beth and I both had tired feet, but we knew we'd complete the race with no problem. When the finish line came into view, Beth looked at me and said, "I'm going to finish this running!" and she took off. Not to be outdone, I thought, *What the heck? My feet couldn't hurt any worse!* and I ran the final fifty yards too.

We finished toward the back of the pack, but it didn't matter. At age sixty-five, I'd accomplished something I wouldn't even have considered before my divorce. What other boundaries could I expand?

Try something new just for fun.

I'd lived in my apartment only a few weeks when I purchased my condo. It was great to have another place to live during the condo renovation while my son and his crew tore out walls, pulled out kitchen cabinets, and ripped up all the flooring.

After they gutted my new condo, I stood in the midst of the construction debris and wondered what I'd done. Normally, I loved to renovate, but now I felt completely dry and void of all creativity. What could I do with this mess now that they'd torn much of it down to the studs and subfloor? Instead of being exhilarated by the opportunity to start with a blank slate, I felt paralyzed and overwhelmed. The demolition scene before me seemed to mirror the current state of my life. What if I couldn't recover that spark that had previously energized and motivated me? Worse yet, what if creativity was no longer part of my life? What if this was simply one more loss to grieve?

That same week, one of my customers invited me to participate in a one-time Saturday morning paper marbling class at a local university. I knew nothing about paper marbling, so I did a bit of research and learned that it's an art form thought to have originated in Turkey about 450 years ago. The process creates beautiful, unique designs like those found on the inside covers of hand-bound books. It intrigued me, so I signed up. The cost was minimal and included all the materials and instruction. I spent three delightful hours with a diverse group of people I'd never met, each there to simply play. It was pure joy.

> *The demolition scene before me seemed to mirror the current state of my life.*

I left the class with fifteen sheets of paper I'd marbled myself, proud of my accomplishments. More than that, I felt a renewed confidence in my abilities to create and decorate my new living space. I returned to the task with enthusiasm, able to make the necessary decisions and relay my vision to the crew who helped me.

I found a colorful rug online to use as a focal point in the living room and started from there. For the next few months, I haunted consignment stores and picked up pieces that spoke to me: a unique curved sofa, a lovely painting for over the fireplace, a small crystal chandelier for my guest bathroom, a ruffled shower curtain. It was fun to watch it all fall into place. I viewed it as part of my therapy, a way to sort and piece together a new picture from the jumbled fragments of my life.

For me, it was important to do this in stages rather than walk into a store and purchase a whole new houseful of furniture at once. It allowed me to process my transition and reorient myself. I needed time to decide what to keep and what to discard, what held meaning and what was merely "stuff," what brought memories of joy and what caused pain. It also opened up a myriad of decorating possibilities, new ways to express myself. When I lived with Glen, I would never have considered the low, aqua leather couch I found in a salvage store, but that piece practically called out, "Buy me! I'm so you!" So, I did, and I love it.

> *I needed time to decide what to keep and what to discard, what held meaning and what was merely "stuff," what brought memories of joy and what caused pain.*

Now my condo is a beautiful and restful expression of my own personality, uniquely mine, and I'm happy I live there. I still have projects to complete, but I remind myself this is a work in progress—a good metaphor for rebuilding my life, a process I expect will continue for a very long time.

Like running a marathon, renovating or decorating your living space is a lovely metaphor for healing and even thriving after a divorce. A word of caution though: Your *pace* and your *place* will both be different from everyone else's. Don't kill yourself trying to keep up.

Chapter 10

ACQUIRING POWER TOOLS

"HEY, CAN I HELP you with that?" The question came from a tall, clean-cut guy who caught up with me in the parking lot as I fought to balance a large box on the cart I pushed out of the hardware store. Normally, I would have waved him off, but I really did need the help, so I took him up on his offer.

"Thanks," I answered. "It's not heavy, just bulky."

He eyed the box as he pushed the cart toward my car. "Is this a gift, or is it for you?"

"Oh, it's for me," I assured him. "I have some projects I'm working on."

His eyes widened, and the slightest hint of amusement played across his face.

"If you don't mind my asking, what kinds of projects do you have that require a twelve-inch miter saw?"

"I'm renovating my condo," I replied. "Tearing out the kitchen, ripping up flooring—that kind of thing. I figure this should be able to handle just about anything."

"You've got that right," he said, but I detected a note of skepticism in his voice.

We reached my Jetta, and it was obvious the box wouldn't fit, even if I laid the seats down.

"I'll take the saw out and put it in the trunk," he said. "Then we can fold up the box. I think it'll fit behind your seat."

The saw filled the trunk side to side and top to bottom, but his plan worked, and I thanked him for his help.

"Good luck with your projects." He saluted me as he stepped away, and again, a slight smile played on his face.

Hmph, I thought. *This guy doesn't think I know anything about tools.*

Over the course of our marriage, Glen and I had owned eight primary residences. We built one house from the ground up, remodeled several others, and did much of the work ourselves. Glen knew a lot about construction and tools. His father was a carpenter and a millwright who taught him well, and in high school, he'd worked for a custom home builder. To his credit, Glen was a good teacher who liked to share his knowledge with me. I'm certainly not an expert, but I know enough about tools to use many of them with confidence.

Perhaps I was overconfident with the miter saw, though. I was pleased with my purchase and had no doubt it was just what I needed. I'd used my husband's ten-inch saw on numerous occasions. The twelve-inch version was on sale for only a few dollars more, and I figured bigger was better. I had no idea a twelve-inch dual-bevel sliding compound miter saw with precision LED shadow guide was a professional tool for large construction jobs—joists, rafters, beams, and such. I confess, in the back of my mind, I might have been thinking, *Nyah, nyah—my saw's bigger than your saw!*

Back home, when I opened my trunk, I realized there was no way I could lift that huge saw by myself. It was much bigger than the ten-inch one I'd used. No worries. My sister Beth would arrive in a few days, and she could help me.

When I showed her the giant tool that gleamed in my trunk, Beth stared at it with the same skeptical look I'd seen on the guy who helped me load it. We managed to lift it out and carry it to the workbench in the garage, where even I could see the saw was ridiculous. We started to laugh and nearly dropped it. Without further discussion, we packed the saw into its box, loaded it into Beth's van, drove back to the store, and exchanged it for a ten-inch model. Fortunately, we didn't run into the guy who'd helped me.

Have I used the saw? Yes, but it wouldn't have been necessary, as my renovation crew provided their own tools. The miter saw wasn't the only item I purchased to stock my workbench. I like do-it-yourself projects, and I'd always had access to whatever hand or power tools I needed. In our divorce, all the tools went with Glen, and I wanted my own supply.

I admit I went overboard. A brief and incomplete inventory of my stash includes screwdrivers, hammers, wrenches, tape measures, a wire cutter, a cordless drill, a hacksaw, a circular saw, a palm sander, several grades of sandpaper, a level or two, a power paint stripper (I'll never use it), a paint sprayer (I don't need that either), a nail gun, an air compressor (borrowed), an electric tile saw, paint brushes and rollers, drop cloths, caulking guns, and various nails, screws, and other fasteners. Someday, I'll have a huge garage sale.

> *All the tools went with Glen, and I wanted my own supply.*

Am I advising you to rush out and get your own tools? Absolutely not! This isn't about tools at all, but I didn't realize that until my mother pointed it out.

"I don't know why I bought all that stuff," I told her after I'd spent the day cleaning my garage. "I'll never use most of it. What made me think I needed all those tools?"

"It wasn't about needing the tools. It was about needing to feel independent and powerful," Mom said. "I knew that all along. It doesn't matter if you never use those power tools. They served their purpose well. They gave you power when you needed it."

Are you good with tools? You can learn. Is there a minor task or repair around the house you can tackle on your own? Even some small exterior accomplishment opens the door to the return of interior power, too.

Chapter 11

ENCOUNTERING SETBACKS

MY COUNSELOR HAD a small heart pillow that hung on the door of her office. Embroidered on it were the words, "Leave your *woulda, coulda, shoulda* at the door!" At one point, she let me borrow it as a reminder that I couldn't go back and change the past.

That mantra remains a valuable piece of advice. You can't go back and alter what's already happened. There are no undo commands or delete buttons for life, no do-overs, regardless of how much you wish for them. Regret can consume a tremendous amount of energy and keep you from moving forward with your life.

As you journey through divorce recovery, it's normal to look back on your marriage and wish you or your spouse had done some things differently. There are times you may get stuck in sadness, anger, or self-pity. When that happens, it's essential to have someone you can call on to help you regain proper perspective. A professional counselor can be

> *Regret can consume a tremendous amount of energy and keep you from moving forward with your life.*

helpful, but it's also important to surround yourself with a support system of family and friends, especially those who've experienced divorce and have re-established "normal" lives. You can be real with people who know, love, and accept you for who you are and who will journey with you through this difficult time.

One of the first people I called about my divorce, even before I informed my children, was a dear friend close to my age who'd been forced to leave her abusive husband years before, taking her five children with her. At least my children were grown. She knew both Glen and me as a couple, and my news stunned and distressed her.

"Oh, Mary Jo, that's so awful!" she cried. She listened to me unload my heartache, and then she blurted out, "You'll make it through this, and someday we'll travel the world together."

That seemingly ludicrous statement somehow buoyed me a bit. She's a master at travel on a shoestring budget and had recently returned from a trip to Singapore with her daughter. With those words, she planted a tiny seed of hope that perhaps my entire life hadn't ended. She's continued to help me focus on God's plan for my life rather than allow me to dwell on the hurt and regret of the past.

I've learned to be selective about the people I include in my support network. Though I love my friends and family dearly, not all of them are suitable partners for this journey. Early on, I found that one of the pitfalls of venting to friends who've gone through divorce is that sometimes my pain seemed to drag them right back into their own post-divorce trauma. Not everyone who moves on has healed enough to listen without reliving their own hurt. Those conversations can deteriorate into ex-spouse-bashing sessions that may, at first, provide a few laughs but end up with all parties feeling grim and dissatisfied.

Give yourself permission to grieve.

There are times grief will sneak up and whack you over the head without warning. Stop and pay attention to it. Don't try to ignore or deny it. Yes, life goes on, but if you pretend nothing is wrong, you build a house of cards. At some point, the whole thing will tumble down.

Much in your marriage was (and is) precious, including your children and all the good times you had, regardless of how it ended. An important part of the lifelong healing process is to accept that there will be times you're keenly aware of this loss. You honor yourself and all that's good and true when you pause to remember, as long as you don't get stuck there.

> *Much in your marriage was (and is) precious . . . regardless of how it ended.*

Nearly two years after my divorce, I had an experience that made me realize I hadn't fully come to terms with my own grief. For some, two years may not seem long at all, but, at that time, I thought I'd successfully moved on with my life. Recently retired, I looked forward to pursuits that included travel, writing, painting, and music. My future lay spread out before me, a sweeping panorama of long-awaited delights, ready to enjoy.

Glen and I had no communication for twenty-two months after our divorce, and though there were still times I missed our life together, I sensed the gaping hole in my heart had begun to fill in around the edges. Then my son told me his father planned to empty a storage unit we'd rented for years and wanted to know what I'd like him to set aside for me. I knew the unit contained at least several boxes of memorabilia, books, two old jewelry boxes, and some art supplies. I'd assumed I'd never see any of those items again, so it was a nice surprise to learn I still had access to them.

It was mid-February, and Glen worked in icy-cold rain for three days to empty the unit. He brought twenty or so boxes to our son's garage, where I could go through them later. When I texted to say I knew it had been a monumental job and I appreciated it, he responded that my thanks meant a lot to him. We exchanged about two dozen texts that night. He commented on finding items like the Christmas china and my old yearbooks; he asked about my health and that of my mother and the rest of my family. He seemed genuinely concerned. Our text conversation was without anger, sarcasm, or bitterness—just two people catching up, very low key. All the while, I wept hot tears, my chest so tight it was hard to breathe, and I missed him so badly I thought I'd die. Much later, I realized it wasn't *him* I missed as much as the good qualities he had, the wonderful times we'd shared, and my sense of emotional security and belonging. I didn't miss the deep deception. I'd always yearned for all the benefits of a loving marriage, and now to be empty-handed—especially so late in life—was a terrible heartache.

Our exchange threw me into two weeks of intense, unexpected grief. I wanted nothing more than to drive over to his house and say, "Let's draw a line from this point forward and start over. Let's hop in the car and go see all the national parks and do all the things we always planned to do!"

I teetered on the edge, ready to throw away every part of the new life I'd pieced together. In my heart of hearts, I knew that would be the wrong decision. I believe we have a moral responsibility to make every effort to reconcile the marriage, but that takes two. If your spouse refuses to cooperate, you're only responsible for your own attitude and efforts. I was still clinging to my dreams, but nothing had changed between us. Any thoughts I had about restoring our relationship were pure fantasy, the product of my own loneliness and longing for the good parts of our life together.

It was time for a reality check. I needed to tap into the support system I'd established over the past two years.

First, I called the same friend who was my initial sounding board—the one who'd fled with her five children and left her abusive husband. I knew she'd gone back many years later to care for him as he was dying of cancer. He'd asked her to marry him again, and she'd nearly agreed until she witnessed his behavior and realized he hadn't changed.

When I told her about my conflicting emotions, she understood completely, and we cried together for the tragedy of losing the men we'd once admired and loved enough to marry. Then we examined the truth of my situation, and I realized my line-in-the-sand approach would likely yield only heartache and frustration. Glen hadn't approached me on bended knee and begged for reconciliation. He'd simply emptied out a storage unit so he could stop paying for it and had done me the courtesy of giving me back my own possessions. It was a bonus to find out we could communicate without malice, and for that I was grateful, but there'd been no fundamental change in his heart or our relationship.

Next, I spoke with the facilitator of the divorce support group I attended at church. Once again, I found strength and encouragement, understanding and validation.

After that conversation, I had an epiphany that jarred me out of my fantasy. I needed to recognize I couldn't expect Glen to change. After all, this was the same man who couldn't be committed to me while we were married. Why would I think he'd be faithful now? I needed to reconcile myself to the possibility he might choose to move on and replace me entirely. That painful realization caused me to admit to my deepest self that our shared life was permanently over. I'd thought I was beyond intense grief, but this seemed as real and painful as what I experienced in the first few months after learning of my husband's infidelity.

When all this happened, I was already in the process of writing this book—perhaps another example of *Look at me, I'm doing so well; let me show you how*. That dose of humility was difficult to swallow, but I've come to understand that others can relate to my vulnerability even more than my success.

Create an appreciation list.

There are days when the losses, challenges, and sorrows of life seem too overwhelming to bear and you want nothing more than to crawl back into bed and pull the covers over your head. Once in a while, it's okay to do that; in fact, it can be therapeutic. However, you can't stay there. Life goes on, and you must find your way back into it.

Sometimes that means you take baby steps—small, deliberate efforts to find reasons to stay in the game. An appreciation list can be a good start. You've probably heard of a gratitude journal, a book you can use to record the things that make you grateful. That's all fine and good, but sometimes that sounds too formal and intimidating, and maybe it's hard for you to feel thankful for anything right now. Instead, start a list on a single sheet of paper or even the back of an envelope.

> *Life goes on, and you must find your way back into it.*

Begin by writing down three of the most basic things that make your life easier or more comfortable, like indoor plumbing, hot water, a microwave. Think about different areas of your life and continue to expand your list: particular friends and family members, music you enjoy, places you like to visit.

This list is only for you. There are no right or wrong answers. You can crumple it up and toss it in the trash if you want. Nobody stands by to judge you. The whole purpose of this exercise is to help you get back into the present moment, to see that there's still some good left in your life, even if the sadness of your divorce has overshadowed it. As you search for reasons to be grateful, your attitude shifts from scarcity to abundance. That allows you to release your fear of loss and open your hands to receive new blessings.

At my lowest point, I recalled a friend who told me she looked for three things that made her happy each day and listed them on her calendar. It didn't matter how big or small they were. She made herself find three things to appreciate every day. I decided to try it. I made note of the sunrise on my way to work, cookies a coworker brought in, a blue heron that flew overhead on my way home. As I became more aware of the gifts around me, I focused less on the losses. The tight, protective shell that encased my pain started to loosen as I began to see the beauty and joy that remained in my life.

But finding and appreciating beauty and joy doesn't end there. All the goods we hold on to so dearly—and appreciate so deeply—will pass away. Let all the things for which you're thankful draw your heart up even higher to the Source of all goodness, security, pleasure, and beauty.

Take charge of your thoughts.

I'm typically on autopilot when I first wake up. Since Glen and I usually showered together, it's not surprising my mind played imaginary conversations during my morning routine nearly every day for the first year after my divorce. The same mental monologue kicked in automatically: I'd address Glen with a few choice terms of endearment, berate him for his behavior, and always end with the unanswerable question, "Why?" The constant mental battle exhausted me, and it set a lousy tone for the rest of the day, but I couldn't seem to break that cycle. Eventually, I stuck the words "Let go" in blue plastic letters on my bathroom mirror, but even that didn't stop the script that played in my head. *Was it me? Why didn't you love me? What's wrong with me?* My ego had taken a huge hit.

One day, as I stepped out of the shower, I heard birds singing outside my bathroom window. Their song was lovely, and I stopped to listen and enjoy it. I realized they'd probably been there many mornings, but I'd been so wrapped up in my imaginary conversations, I'd failed to hear God's beautiful music. What else had I missed when I allowed negative, unproductive thoughts to hijack my mind? Maybe it was time to make a conscious effort to control my thoughts rather than relinquish that power to forces that always led me into a downward spiral.

I resolved to fight back and be intentional in my thinking and mindful of my surroundings. I tried to engage my senses during my morning ritual. A shower, soap, lotion, cosmetics—all these add up to a very sensual experience when I don't drift into autopilot. Imaginary conversations can't kick in as easily if I stay aware of my environment. When they do invade, I consciously re-route my thoughts to the luxury of warm water on my skin, the fragrance of my shampoo, the softness of the towel. Sometimes I add music to the experience, but I continue to listen for the birds that sing outside my window.

> *What else had I missed when I allowed negative, unproductive thoughts to hijack my mind?*

Any type of abandonment or betrayal is a deep wound to your sense of self. To face reality with humility requires supernatural grace. Ask God for as much as you need. Let beauty be a salve for your soul.

Chapter 12

COPING WITH ISOLATION, LONELINESS, AND LOSS OF IDENTITY

YOU'RE PRECIOUS TO GOD. He knows every tear you shed, every longing of your heart. God loves you as if you're the only one. He made you in His image and likeness. You've existed for all eternity in the mind of God, and your life on earth is not an accident or mistake. Your true identity lies outside of any human relationship, including your marriage. God loves you unconditionally, and no human being can take that away from you.

How do I know this? Over a ten-year period during my marriage, I wrote a series of Scripture-based essays about the beauty and sacredness of married love as a personal path to holiness. I'd compiled these into a book, approved by my local bishop, and was ready to publish it when the sudden derailment of my own marriage caused me to set it aside.

> *Your true identity lies outside of any human relationship, including your marriage.*

After my divorce, I thought I no longer had any credibility on the subject of marriage or related topics. But the message remains intact even if the messenger is broken. Truth remains truth. My divorce doesn't diminish my appreciation of the importance of marriage. Nor does it negate the central message I learned through writing about married love.

Marriage and the one-flesh union of a husband and a wife are the visible sign of God's love in the world, the most sacred relationship in creation, and the basic structure of civilization. The title of my book on marriage was *In the Arms of My Beloved*. You might suppose *My Beloved* means my husband, but that's not the case. When I wrote that book, I learned that married love is a reflection of the perfect love God has for each one of us. We're each uniquely beloved by God. To God, each one is the only one. That's the message I wanted to convey.

After my divorce, I grieved the loss of my book nearly as much as I did the breakup of my marriage. I'd spent years reading and writing about married love as a way to connect with God. Had it all been in vain? Where was God now? Had my relationship with Him changed? What did it look like now that my marriage had crumbled?

> *We're each uniquely beloved by God. To God, each one is the only one.*

I went back to Scripture, and this time, I read through the lens of one betrayed by my earthly spouse. I found clear evidence that those of us who've experienced divorce haven't lost our relationship with God. In fact, God seems to speak comfort directly to us:

> *The Lord calls you back,*
>   *like a wife forsaken and grieved in spirit,*
> *A wife married in youth and then cast off,*
>   *says your God* (Isaiah 54:6).

For he who has become your husband is your Maker;
his name is the Lord of Hosts . . . (Isaiah 54:5).

The Lord is close to the brokenhearted;
and those who are crushed in spirit he saves (Psalm 34:19).

Though the mountains leave their place
and the hills be shaken,
My love shall never leave you . . .
O afflicted one, storm-battered and unconsoled . . . (Isaiah 54:10–11).

My wanderings you have counted;
my tears are stored in your flask;
are they not recorded in your book? (Psalm 56:9)

My husband's final betrayal after forty-four years of marriage devastated me, but it wasn't the first time I'd experienced that kind of grief. When I was thirty-one years old, I walked in on a phone conversation I was never meant to hear between Glen and another woman. When I asked him if my world was about to fall apart, he assured me their relationship was purely platonic, that they were only friends. I wanted to believe him, but in my heart, I feared what I'd heard was more than friendship. I felt as if my foundation had collapsed. Life no longer seemed to hold any joy.

Somehow, I knew we'd work through this, and it seemed we had—our life together lasted thirty-three more years. Looking back, I realize we didn't "work through" it, though. Glen ignored it and acted as if it hadn't happened, and I buried it. I told no one. The shame was unbearable, and I didn't want our family and friends to think any less of Glen or me. As a result, I was miserable and depressed much of the time, irritable and impatient with my children. To fight my depression, I over-volunteered in church and other activities. I didn't know it then, but instead of hiding or minimizing my pain, I should have sought professional help. Instead, I toughed it out for two years and cried every morning after Glen left for work.

Finally, one evening, as we rushed to leave for a camping trip—running behind as usual—I yelled at my two young children and my husband, "We're not going tonight! Get out of my sight and go to bed!" All three of them scrambled and left me alone. I plopped down on the sofa with my head in my hands, feeling numb and wretched, unloving and unlovable. I wanted nothing more than to be swallowed up, to disappear and relieve myself and my family of such misery.

In my desolation, I became aware of a warm, loving Presence that surrounded me and permeated my entire being. I knew instinctively this Presence was God. I felt no condemnation, no need to measure up or perform, just gentle acceptance of me in my miserable condition. My tears flowed as I sat bathed in this love and forgiveness. I no longer felt connected to the multiple distractions and obligations that had pulled me in so many directions a short time before. I was conscious only of the overwhelming love that enveloped me.

As I sat there, I understood that God loves me unconditionally and without measure—and not only does God love me that way, He has that same love for every person He's ever created, without exception. God, who *is* Love, can't *not* love.

It was, and is, more than I could fathom, but that truth remains at the core of my relationship with God and my understanding of who I am in God's sight. In the many years since that experience, I've been tempted to doubt God's love, to go back to thinking I must earn it, that I must try harder, that I'm not worthy. The truth is, we can't earn God's love. None of us is good enough, no matter how hard we try. None of us is worthy. God loves us, not *despite* the fact that we're human, but *because* of it.

That truth has armed me in the attack against my marriage and my very self, though it's an ongoing battle.

I want to share that same truth with you. Nothing can change the fact that God loves you more than you can ever know. Yes, the pain of losing the love of your earthly spouse is agonizing and intense. The wounds are deep and lasting. Heartbreak is aptly named.

It would be nice if peeling away your spouse would reveal this shiny new layer of God's unconditional love to comfort and console you. I wish that were the case. The process of healing after divorce is more like the formation of thin, fragile scabs and tender pink scar tissue that can easily be torn and disrupted.

> *God loves us, not* despite *the fact that we're human, but* because *of it.*

We tend to identify ourselves in multiple roles as wife or husband, daughter or son, mother or father, employee, business owner, caregiver, volunteer, etc., but what we *do* doesn't define who we *are*. All those roles—as good as they are—are finite and temporary, changeable by choice or circumstances beyond our control.

We're also likely to define ourselves by how other people see us, and to measure our worth compared to those around us: *Am I thin enough? Am I smart enough? Am I pretty enough? Do I make enough money? Do my wrinkles make me look old?* Add a spouse's betrayal and infidelity to all those ingredients, and you have the perfect recipe for a self-esteem of zero, a true identity crisis.

The real you—the person God sees and loves without conditions or expectations—is someone only you can discover. Although your divorce strips you of a major portion of your identity, it leaves room to discover or re-discover who you really are.

Who are you at the essential, unchangeable core of yourself? This is a truth we must each discover. Most of us have spent a lifetime wrapping layer upon layer to shape and reshape ourselves to fit various molds at different stages of life. The adult we become seldom resembles the child who began that journey.

The bare, raw condition in which you find yourself after divorce can be an opportunity to peer beneath those layers and allow some aspects of that child to emerge, free from the expectations and constraints imposed by your marriage. Think of it as a gift in ugly packaging.

> *Who are you at the essential, unchangeable core of yourself? This is a truth we must each discover.*

Of course, this isn't an instant process. For me, it's continued to evolve over the years since my divorce. Some changes are small, almost imperceptible. Others are milestones. Many times, my journey feels like three steps forward, two back—or even two steps forward, four back. Just about the time I think I have it all together, I'm hit with some reminder that recovery is a lifelong task.

After my divorce, I didn't see Glen for over two years. Since we both lived in the same city, I knew there was always a chance I might run into him. No matter where I went—to the grocery store, Walmart, out to dinner—I was always on the lookout for him. I felt I had to look my best, with my hair, makeup, and clothes just right. "See?" I wanted to be able to say if I saw him. "I'm doing great! Don't you wish you still had me in your life?"

I knew those thoughts and behaviors weren't reasonable, but I couldn't seem to get beyond them. Besides, caring about my appearance actually made me feel better, so it wasn't all bad. On a deeper level, though, I recognized I was allowing my fear of not measuring up to control me. I'd made my spouse's view of me more important than how God saw me. Marriage and family relationships are blessings, but they're never meant to take first place in our hearts. When they do, what's meant to be good then becomes a "god."

My fear came to a head one year on my son's birthday. Born on July 5, my son has always regarded his birthday as a community celebration, complete with Fourth of July fireworks. Even as an adult, he's invited friends and family to share in the fun each year. For the first two years after the divorce, he didn't invite me to that party. He didn't intend to hurt me; in fact, I'd suggested the arrangement. I shared Christmas Eve with my son and his family; his dad could attend the birthday party. Still, it didn't sit well with me, and I secretly resented being excluded.

The third year, to my surprise, he invited both of us. I thought and prayed about whether to attend and concluded that this was an opportunity to encounter Glen under controlled circumstances. If it went well, maybe I'd no longer feel so anxious about running into him. If it didn't go well, I could just leave.

The day arrived, and I faced the party with both dread and anticipation. As I pulled into my son's driveway, I caught a glimpse of Glen as he walked toward the house. I purposely dawdled at my car until I was sure he'd gone inside. We're an affectionate bunch, and my entry prompted hugs from my son, my daughter-in-law, my granddaughter, and some of their friends. I could see Glen standing in a corner of the kitchen.

"Well, hello there," he greeted me.

He looked much better than the last time I'd seen him. In the year prior to our divorce, he'd decided to stop shaving and had usually worn his "landlord" clothes—a ratty flannel shirt and torn jeans. Now, his hair and beard were neatly trimmed. He wore a light blue polo shirt and new beige cargo shorts. His sandals looked fresh from the box.

"Hi," I managed to respond.

I turned my attention to the food and carried a salad to the table. The awkwardness between us eased a bit as we all sat down to eat. We both participated in the general conversation but said little to each other. Eventually, he asked about my mother, and I gave some polite answers. We were civil and well-behaved.

After dessert, I saw an opportunity to make my exit. Again, we repeated hugs all around. There was a moment of uneasy hesitation when I looked across the room at Glen.

"It was nice to see you," I said. Then I added, "You look good."

He jerked his head back. "Well, thank you!"

With that, I tilted my chin up ever so slightly and walked out the door. All the way home (only two miles), I congratulated myself: *Well done. Mission accomplished. You did it!*

Only when I was alone in my bed did I allow my grief to pour out in a torrent of tears, to mourn yet again my terrible loss.

I realized the full impact of this event the next day, when I was in the middle of a messy home improvement project. Dressed in an old T-shirt and tattered cutoff jeans, I didn't hesitate to run out to the hardware store as is. So what if I ran into him now? I no longer felt controlled by the need to look good for someone whose opinion should no longer matter to me. I'd faced my fear and survived. It was time to move on.

Have you given someone you love the power to control how you think and feel about yourself? It can be a hard habit to break.

Chapter 13

KEEPING YOUR GUARD UP

DIVORCE WASN'T PART of my paradigm, and I didn't choose it lightly. I'm blessed to have been surrounded by long-term marriages my whole life. My parents were married nearly sixty-five years before my dad died, my grandparents celebrated their sixty-sixth anniversary, and my husband's parents were married for sixty-three years. Though each couple occasionally bickered, their mutual love was clear to everyone around them. After forty-four years, I had little reason to suspect my own marriage wouldn't follow the same path.

When you've been married a long time, it's difficult to separate your identity from that of your spouse. The thought of life alone, without that person by your side, can frighten and overwhelm you. It's tempting to seek out someone to fill that void, especially if you based much of your own self-image and self-worth on your marriage relationship. Sometimes it seems easier to replace than to recover, to jump into a romantic relationship or

> *The thought of life alone, without that person by your side, can frighten and overwhelm you.*

even a short-term fling while you're still reeling from the devastation of your divorce.

I might have fallen into that trap, but I wanted to be faithful. As a Catholic, I believe only death and not civil divorce can end a true marriage, and I wasn't ready to investigate annulment.

I'd also heard personal horror stories from several friends—some newly widowed, some divorced—who'd thrown caution to the wind and ended up regretting what had started out as just a good time with a fun guy. Their fiascoes usually involved alcohol.

It's a different world out there. Regardless of how self-sufficient and independent you are, if you were married for more than fifteen years or so, you'll probably be quite surprised by the differences in the dating game since the last time you played it. All the advice and warnings you might have given to your teenage children now apply to you. Unfortunately, there are some people who'll assume you're ready to hop into bed after two or three dates; others are openly predatory. Sad to say, you need to keep your guard up.

As a former business owner, I was comfortable with male friends and business acquaintances, and as a parish nurse, I'd helped both men and women work through grief issues. So, when an older gentleman I knew, whose wife had Alzheimer's disease, told me he needed someone to talk to and asked if we could meet somewhere, I readily agreed. At first, he suggested coffee, then changed it to dinner at an Italian restaurant the following evening. I thought that sounded too much like a date and wanted to change the venue back to a coffee shop, but I couldn't reach him by phone, so I decided to keep my commitment. After all, he was nearly eighty years old and just having a difficult time coping with his wife's illness . . . right?

When I arrived at the restaurant, he stood ready to greet me at the entrance.

"Ah, the first of our many hugs!" he exclaimed as he reached out and embraced me. I stiffened at his fresh cologne and his firm kiss on my cheek. Obviously, the two of us weren't on the same wavelength.

He escorted me to our table and ordered a glass of wine for himself. I declined. Then he ordered mussels and mentioned they were aphrodisiacs. I thought to myself, *It'll take a lot more than that*, and ordered a pizza.

I tried to steer the conversation to his wife and family, but he spent most of an hour expounding on his experience as a government agent. Occasionally, he'd say something like, "But enough about me. I want to know about you!" and then continue right on telling me about his exploits.

He did ask me a few pointed questions about my marriage and the reason for my divorce. "Well, you didn't withhold sex from him, did you?" I bristled a bit at that but didn't let it show.

He finally voiced the real reason he wanted to meet. "I'm very virile," he said. "My wife has been in a nursing home for five years. I'm looking for love and affection."

At that moment, I wished I were the type of woman who could upend the table, toss his glass of wine in his face, pour the mussels into his lap, and storm out. But I'm not. I'm a nice girl who thinks she has to be polite and kind, even in situations that don't merit it.

"Well," I began. "Even though I'm divorced, I consider marriage to be very sacred, and, at this point, I still think of myself as married in God's eyes. I know it must be really hard to keep your marriage vows when your wife has been ill for so long, but I'm not willing to have that kind of relationship with you."

I really wanted to scream, "I'm six months out of a divorce after my husband betrayed me, and you want me to be the other woman while your wife is dying in a nursing home? ARE YOU KIDDING ME?!" But I didn't. His attitude cooled, and he thanked me for my honesty. I thanked him for dinner, and we walked out of the restaurant together.

I waited in my car until I was sure he'd driven away. Then I called my mother and sobbed, "I'm so angry! I have no frame of reference for this. I'm completely naive. I used to take people at face value, and now I can't. I hate this!"

At some point, we both started to laugh. Here I was, sixty-five years old, crying about a date to my eighty-five-year-old mother, just as if I were a teenager. I realized that after being married for forty-four years to my childhood sweetheart, I was completely green and vulnerable regarding the dating scene.

My new rule: I'll go out with mixed groups of men and women, but not one-on-one with the opposite sex. I've discovered there are other people like me who like to get out once in a while and enjoy a good time without the pressure of dating. A friend introduced me to a local network of mixed sixty-something singles who host casual outings like attending a free summer concert, touring small art galleries, listening to a live group at a pub, or going to breakfast together on Saturday mornings. I've been to several events. There was no pressure to pair up, and the conversation was relaxed and genuine. I heard no talk about ex-wives or ex-husbands, no bitter or sarcastic references, and no self-pity. That, in itself, was refreshing and energizing. But I realize I still have to be careful. Just because *I'm* not looking for a date, I can't assume the true intentions of the other person.

As a post-script to this anecdote, I ran into that man a few months later, after avoiding him on several occasions.

I knew his wife had finally died, and I asked how he was doing. He told me her funeral had been beautiful, a fitting tribute to such a good wife and mother. Then he teared up, looked me in the eye, and said, "I need to thank you. I think you know why."

"You've walked a difficult journey," I answered, and left it at that.

If you're tempted to mask your loneliness and pain by "replacing," ask God for the grace to be whole in His love.

Chapter 14

LEARNING TO FORGIVE

FORGIVENESS. Maybe you choke on that word. You're certainly not alone. And yet, it's necessary to forgive if you want to find peace and healing after divorce. However, forgiveness isn't what most people think it is.

Forgiveness isn't a feeling. It's an act of the will, a free choice. It's not a one-time event, but, rather, an ongoing process, a series of baby steps, a state of the heart, a journey with stops and starts.

I think there are several distinct stages to the process of forgiving someone who's severely wounded you. I base this solely on my own experience and not on any formal or even informal research. Some of this may sound harsh, but I'm being honest about my gut-level feelings and responses as I've worked to forgive my husband. Your experience may be different, but this has been my journey:

Stage 1. Shock and bewilderment

Initially, I was too crushed to fight back or even think about revenge. I simply wanted to leave the man who'd betrayed me so completely. I told him he'd taken something very beautiful and fragile and smashed it, and I couldn't put the pieces back together. I remember saying, "Not as a punishment, but as a consequence, I can't stay in this relationship any longer."

That sounds very calm and rational, and, at the time, it was, although my heart was broken and I sobbed as I said those words to him. Part of me still wanted Glen to hold me and say he was sorry and he'd never betray me again. That's not what happened. He remained a cold stranger who responded without emotion: "Well, I do love you. I'm sorry you feel that way, but I do understand." *Really?!*

A few nights later, I moved into absolute rage and indignation.

Stage 2. Desiring personal revenge

At 4:00 a.m., I marched out to the living room, where Glen was asleep on the sofa. How dare he sleep while I lay awake and agonized about the breakup of our marriage? I loomed over him and shrieked at the top of my lungs, "I want you out of here! You'd better leave now, or I'm going to hurt you!"

Jarred out of a sound sleep, he stared at me as if I were a madwoman (and at that moment, I was). He grabbed some clothes, jumped into his truck, and didn't come back to the house for several days. I was satisfied with his response.

Perhaps *revenge* is too strong a word. *Vindication* is more like it. I really wouldn't have physically hurt him, but part of me wanted him to feel the same pain he'd inflicted on me.

> *Part of me wanted him to feel the same pain he'd inflicted on me.*

It's easy to become stuck at this stage. There's a lot of energy and positive feedback that come from self-righteous anger. I felt the need to hang on to my hurt for a while—to take it out and examine it, hold it in my hands and turn it around, to look at it from all angles, as if it were a physical thing with form and weight and color and texture and smell. I had no desire or inclination to forgive my husband. I was right, and he was wrong, and that was all there was to it.

Stage 3. Calling on God's justice

Eventually, I realized I couldn't stoke that anger forever. It poisoned me; it raised my blood pressure and endangered my physical and mental health. But it was hard to give it up. When I took anger out of the equation, all that remained was sadness, and sadness didn't give me energy. It took it away.

I decided to hand Glen over to God. Yes, that's right, I'd let God put him in his place. I didn't want God to condemn him to hell, although that desire might be part of this stage, and I can understand anyone who has those thoughts. No, I'd let God mete out whatever justice He deemed appropriate. I didn't actively wish my husband harm, but I didn't exactly pray for him to be blessed, either.

You can find plenty of support for this mindset in the Old Testament, particularly the Book of Psalms, so it's tempting to stay in this mode. Evidently, it wasn't common to pray for your enemies back then.

Early on, I knew I needed spiritual advice and help to handle my anger and unforgiveness, so I requested an appointment with one of the priests at my parish. To my chagrin, the only one available was Father Stan, a Polish priest I didn't know well. To me, he'd always seemed very serious and, I assumed, quite conservative. I stormed into his office and poured out my story, half expecting to be pushed into marriage counseling and told to forgive. Instead, this wise and compassionate man listened to me rant and then gave me some very practical, down-to-earth advice: "Forgiveness doesn't mean you forget and act as if this hasn't happened. You live now for your children and your grandchildren. You decide what the rules should be, and you make the rules. You must be strong! Be very good to yourself. This stress can hurt you, make you sick, even kill you, so you must take care of yourself. Eat good food and rest today and tomorrow. Then make your decisions and your rules."

> *Forgiveness doesn't mean you forget and act as if this hasn't happened.*

He spent well over an hour with me. I felt validated and less out of control. He listened to me and didn't dismiss my emotions or give me pat answers. He confirmed that this was a cataclysmic break in my marriage and helped me realize I could make choices. I went home more at peace, with the beginnings of a sense of direction and empowerment.

Stage 4. Calling on God's mercy

Jesus clearly calls us to love our enemies: "Forgive us our trespasses as we forgive those who trespass against us." I hated to think of Glen as my enemy, but during our divorce, that became the only way I could define our relationship. As I tried to pray for strength and help, I began to realize I had to release my anger, my need for an apology, and my desire for retaliation. Instead of calling on God to exact His justice for me, I knew I had to pray for His mercy and forgiveness for both Glen and myself.

Stage 5. Embracing forgiveness

Forgiveness is ultimately a personal decision. It takes great courage to surrender your desire for revenge and move toward an attitude of mercy, but to do so frees you from anger and resentment and allows your healing process to begin.

Another priest advised me, "Don't let this turn you into someone you don't want to be." I needed to hear that. My bitterness had begun to show up as a sarcastic edge, an attempt to veil my pain with dark humor. Sometimes it popped out when I didn't expect it, usually as a derogatory remark about Glen. It wasn't attractive, to say the least.

When you forgive someone who harmed you, it doesn't mean you accept their unacceptable behavior or negate the injury. Your refusal to forgive seems at first to be a way to wield power over the person who injured you, but it actually means you allow that person to continue to control you. A popular truism says that not forgiving is like drinking poison and then waiting for the other person to die.

Forgiveness is unilateral. It doesn't depend on an apology from the person who hurt you, no matter how much you want to hear those words. Being wronged by another person is never easy to bear. Some violations seem unforgivable, and, indeed, you may not be able to forgive on your own.

> *Not forgiving is like drinking poison and then waiting for the other person to die.*

When your pain is so intense you think you can't forgive, you can call on Jesus, who lives in you, to forgive the other person for you. You may not feel any different, but trust that God is at work and continue to thank Him for it. His forgiveness is genuine, and it's yours for the asking.

"Get real," you're probably saying.

That truth is as real as it gets—and also as difficult. This is where the rubber meets the road for all of us who consider ourselves Christians.

Forgiveness is an act of the will, a decision we may need to make over and over again. Sometimes it's easy to forgive. More often it requires hard work and persistent effort. While it's not healthy to bury and ignore the hurt and anger we experience when someone wounds us, it's even more destructive to allow unforgiveness to fester and ferment inside us.

The desire to nurse our wounds can quickly become a tool of the enemy, who fans the flames of righteous indignation until they blind and consume us. It's very tempting to hang on to our pain and the desire for revenge or retaliation. It feels so right. But we'll never be free ourselves until we release that hurt and anger.

> *Forgiveness is an act of the will, a decision we may need to make over and over again.*

Long before my divorce, I experienced the need to forgive two different people for serious injuries. In the first case, a close friend had lied to me for over twenty years about a very grave and confidential matter. When he called one day to confess the truth and ask for my forgiveness, I was so shocked, I felt physically ill, as if someone had pressed a fast-forward button inside me. I told him I didn't know how to handle what he'd told me and hung up.

I knew I couldn't deal with it on my own, so I poured out my confusion in a plea to God: "Lord, this is too much for me. I don't think I can forgive him. I don't know what to do with this."

I pictured myself at the foot of the cross. How could I ever seek forgiveness if I couldn't offer it myself? "Lord, I want to forgive him, but I can't do this on my own. I need Your grace. Jesus, help me to forgive him and to love him for Your sake. I don't *feel* love for him now, but I release my anger and hurt to you, and I pray for Your perfect will to be done in his life."

To my amazement, I felt instant peace. My confusion and the out-of-control sensation that had gripped me disappeared. My healing was complete and immediate. I forgave him at once, called him back to reconcile, and have never felt anything but love toward him since.

The second example is one I've already mentioned—when I was thirty-one and walked in on the phone call between my husband and another woman. In that case, I handed my unforgiveness over to God every day for two years before I finally surrendered it and ceased to grab it back. When we wrestle with unforgiveness, it's sometimes necessary to seek the help of a trusted professional or a spiritual director. In retrospect, it might have been easier had I done so. I view that long, painful struggle as dying to self. If only that were a one-time exercise!

I heard a young nun from Louisiana teach this vivid analogy for unforgiveness:

Imagine you're a small child. You watch your mother as she changes your baby brother's soiled diaper. You see her remove the dirty diaper and throw it into the pail. She gently and carefully cleanses the baby's bottom and washes away all the excrement and odor. Then she applies soothing, sweet-smelling lotion or powder and dresses the baby in fresh, clean garments. When she's finished, your mother kisses the baby, places him in the crib, and leaves the room.

You think, *What a mess that baby made! He doesn't deserve all that love and attention. I'll fix that.* You march over to the diaper pail, fish out the dirty, stinky diaper, and place it right back on the baby.

That's what we do when we choose to hang on to our own unforgiveness instead of asking God to minister to and forgive the other person.

To take it one step further, imagine yourself as the little baby. When we don't forgive ourselves after we've sought and received God's mercy and forgiveness, it's as if we slap that cold, dirty, poopy diaper right back on our own bodies!

Learning to forgive is a process that takes place between you and God. You're safe in the arms of the One who knows the truth about you, your spouse, and your marriage.

Chapter 15

BECOMING THE PERSON GOD CREATED YOU TO BE

*I will espouse you to me forever:
I will espouse you in right and in justice,
in love and in mercy;
I will espouse you in fidelity,
and you shall know the Lord*
(Hosea 2:21-22).

THAT VERSE takes my breath away. Just think—although your earthly marriage was flawed by sin and human weakness, your relationship with Jesus as your True Spouse is an everlasting love. He invites you to enter into an intimate, ever-deepening marriage with the One who created you and knows everything about you. No more failing to measure up to someone else's expectations. No more worrying that you're not good enough or pretty enough or smart enough. God says, "You're enough, just as you are. Forever. Period. I've already

> *God says, "You're enough, just as you are. Forever. Period."*

proven My love by dying to rescue you! Lift your face and let Me love you!"

My friend, Tara, had been divorced for eight years when I first met her. Her husband was a verbally abusive bully throughout their entire marriage. When it became obvious he was having affairs with multiple women, even his friends had urged her to leave him. She told me she'd been sexually abused as a child and had stayed with her husband because she didn't think she deserved anything better. She hated him and confessed she was unable to pray the *Our Father* because she still couldn't forgive him, even eight years later.

Initially, Tara was timid and reserved, reluctant to participate in conversation except to talk about how mean and rotten her ex-husband had been. She seemed stuck, a victim of her unhappy past. In an effort to leave that behind, she started to see a therapist and joined a divorce support group.

As she progressed through therapy, Tara blossomed. She began to see herself as worthy of love and happiness. She learned to release the guilt and shame she'd carried for most of her life, and she discovered a joy that bubbled up from deep inside her. Tara stopped thinking of her bad marriage as punishment and began to understand her true relationship with God. It was difficult for her to accept that God loved her unconditionally since she'd never experienced that type of love from anyone else. Little by little, she learned to trust in God's love and mercy, to forgive herself, and to let go of the anger and unforgiveness she harbored toward her former husband and others who'd hurt her so deeply.

Tara's transformation was remarkable. She became more outgoing and talkative, and she spoke with enthusiasm about her future. Her smile was contagious, and her mischievous sense of humor made it fun to be around her.

"You just radiate joy," I told her one day.

She responded, "I'm finally free! I decided to forgive my husband, and I gave all my hurt to God. I know God loves me, and that changes everything!"

Are *you* stuck? Divorce is only one part of your life experience. Sometimes, it's the tipping point, though—the wound that injures you so badly you can no longer cope with past hurts you've buried or ignored. There's no stigma in seeking help. You want your wounds to heal, not fester and infect your whole being.

Chapter 16

LETTING GOD'S LOVE SHINE THROUGH YOU

BEAUTIFUL STAINED GLASS church windows have always filled me with awe and wonder. The play of light streaming through the different colors presents an almost other-worldly experience—not surprising, since the original purpose of such windows was to create a heavenly light that would depict the presence of God. In the Middle Ages, when most of the population of Europe was illiterate, these windows also became the "poor man's Bible," illustrating stories from the Old and New Testaments and the lives of the saints—sermons in light and color.

My daughter shares my fascination with stained glass. Because we live far apart and she has a heavy work schedule, we don't often get to see each other. In late 2019, I found inexpensive flights to Paris and proposed that we meet there for a week at Christmastime. To my delight, she agreed. It was a new experience for both of us. One of the highlights of our trip was Sainte-Chapelle, King (Saint) Louis IX's royal chapel completed in 1248, originally built to house sacred relics of Christ's Passion, including the Crown of Thorns. Though not nearly as large as the Cathedral of Notre Dame, this chapel boasts 1,113 spectacular scenes in fifteen towering, spire-like windows that are perhaps the world's finest examples of Gothic stained glass artwork.

As you can tell, I like words, but I have no words to describe the exquisite beauty of that chapel. It left me speechless. I knew I was in the presence of something only God could have inspired. The day was sunny, and sparkling multi-colored light poured in through every window. Well, nearly every window. You see, there's one entire panel that's dull and dark because an adjacent building, constructed much later, butts up against it and shuts out the sunlight. Without light from outside, the entire window remains lifeless and colorless, unable to fulfill its original purpose.

The grief and pain of divorce sometimes threaten to block the grace of God in our lives, much like the wall that prevents light from flowing through that window. We feel dull and lifeless, without joy or color.

But God's love is stronger than our pain, and there's nothing that can block that love. We're each created to be a unique expression of God's love. No one else can fulfill the purpose God has for each one of us, and divorce doesn't change that. It may take time to discover, rediscover, or reframe your purpose, but it hasn't disappeared.

Each of us has a particular God-given call to bring grace into the world—to transmit that grace into our family, our workplace, our church—to everyone we meet, everywhere we go. We do that when we share ourselves as gift to one another. This is the basis for marriage, but married love is certainly not the only way to live it out.

Every interaction with another human being is an opportunity to both embody and encounter the living Christ. If we remember that—and I often fail to do so—we'll find ourselves surprised by how often we can bless and be blessed by others. Our daily interactions, even with people we don't know, can have profound and lasting effects and bring us great happiness and fulfillment.

One day when I felt particularly lonely and sad, I attended morning Mass. I was new in the area and didn't know anyone in the church, which added to my sense of isolation. At the sign of peace, the older gentleman next to me reached for my hand. Instead of releasing it, as I expected, he held it for several minutes as Mass continued. Perhaps his gesture was a habit, meant for a wife no longer present with him. I only know his kind touch felt very personal and comforting, almost as if God was telling me He knew my sorrow and sent someone to show me He cared. I still remember this simple encounter years later, and it continues to bless and console me.

> *Our daily interactions, even with people we don't know, can have profound and lasting effects and bring us great happiness and fulfillment.*

God sends grace into the world through you. When you're at your best, what are five ways you sparkle and shine?

Chapter 17

SEEKING CONTINUOUS IMPROVEMENT

I'VE ALWAYS LOVED the water. Having spent my childhood in the Arizona desert, I appreciate the beautiful lakes and rivers of the Midwest, where I've lived for much of my adult life. Glen and I owned boats throughout most of our marriage, and much of our family fun revolved around time at the lake. Our children rode in the ski boat from the time they were infants and loved overnight campouts on the pontoon or summer weekends at our friends' lake house.

The last boat my husband and I owned was a twenty-six-foot 1979 Carver Santa Cruz, a yacht by some standards. It was thirty years old when we acquired it, and it was definitely a project, a true labor of love. We christened it *Continuous Improvement*, a tongue-in-cheek reference to Glen's career as a quality engineer, and, as any boat owner will tell you, an appropriate name for what can become a floating money pit. We were lucky. Beyond the initial work and capital we poured into its restoration, our boat performed well most of the time.

Continuous Improvement stood an imposing twelve feet high on the trailer we used to transport her from our house to one of several lakes we liked to visit. We attracted stares and interest from onlookers each time we went through our two-person routine to launch what was often the largest boat on the lake. Both of us liked to cruise at a relaxed pace on a Friday evening and then anchor out in a cove so we could enjoy some wine and gaze at the stars before we spent the night in the comfortable berth inside the boat's cabin.

There was something so soothing about sleeping on the water—the gentle rocking of the boat, the night sounds of crickets chirping on the shore, the occasional fish slapping the surface. It made me feel totally safe and protected. I could relax better there than anywhere else.

After my divorce, I knew it was unlikely I'd ever have that kind of experience again. It wasn't practical for me to own a boat big enough to sleep on, and, besides, I wouldn't feel safe by myself overnight on the water. I set that part of my life aside and counted it among the many losses I needed to grieve.

But my new condo changed all that. It's a second-story walk-up that overlooks an eighty-acre spring-fed lake that's clear and deep. Each condo has dock access. From the moment I saw the lake, I could picture myself lounging on a small pontoon boat, a soft breeze blowing, a book in my hand. Just to imagine it felt soothing and relaxing.

I did some research and found exactly what I wanted: an inexpensive, lightweight, six-foot-by-twelve-foot basic pontoon called the AquaCraft Little River Boat, built and sold by a family in Wisconsin. I ordered one online, and they delivered it within a month.

My son and his friends carried my new boat down to the lake and attached the electric trolling motor and battery. I added a solar cell to charge the battery (you can learn anything via the internet!), outfitted the boat with four yellow plastic lawn chairs, raised the bright blue canopy, and set off across the lake just as I'd imagined. It was glorious!

I named my little boat *Just Be* and added the words "Choose Joy" in yellow letters along the side. It became a symbol of my new life, my decision to move forward and discover new joys to savor.

> *My little boat became a symbol of my new life, my decision to move forward and discover new joys to savor.*

Although I don't sleep on my boat, I still experience that same peaceful sensation every night before I slip into bed. From my bedroom window, I look out onto the lake and take in the beauty of the lights that reflect on its surface. As I breathe a prayer of thanks for this gift that feeds my soul, I can feel my whole being relax. It's as if I hear God say, "I created all this just for you."

You don't know the future, but God does, and He will see you through it. He still gives you lots of freedom to make choices—and sometimes that can be scary. But *draw* close to Him, *stay* close to Him, and *enjoy* your life. Believe me: the best is yet to come!

FIFTEEN ACTIONS TO HELP YOU MOVE FROM BROKEN TO WHOLE

1. Work out anger in a safe physical manner.
2. Take time to reboot.
3. Ask God to show you His truth.
4. Acknowledge the end of the life you shared with your spouse.
5. Know that God journeys with you and shares your pain.
6. Exercise regularly, get adequate rest, take good care of your general health.
7. Communicate your needs and set boundaries as necessary.
8. Break the news in your own way.
9. Get in touch with nature.
10. Try something new just for fun.
11. Give yourself permission to grieve.
12. Create an appreciation list.
13. Take charge of your thoughts.
14. Take baby steps toward forgiveness.
15. Open yourself to God's love and healing grace.

ACKNOWLEDGMENTS

I'VE BEEN A WRITER since childhood, but I never dreamed I'd author a book about divorce—especially my own. This work isn't complete until I express my gratitude to the people who've helped me along this journey. Though there are too many to name here, each one is a shining jewel I treasure. My sincere thanks to all of you:

JoAnn Rennert, my mother, for "sticking around" to cry, listen, and laugh with me. Your wisdom and friendship are invaluable. I'm proud to be your daughter.

My father, *Bob Rennert*, the best man I've ever known, for continuing to watch over me even now. I love you, Dad.

My children, *Lisa* and *John*, for your love and support. You are and always have been my greatest joy and my grandest adventure, in the best sense of the word.

My daughter-in-law, *Anna*, for your love and advice and for helping me pack, unpack, and repack more times than either of us wants to remember.

My sisters, *Susie* (you brought bubbles!) and *Beth* (you went the extra mile, literally!), and my brother, *Rob*. We've been through a lot together and found laughter in most of it. You're amazing warriors, and I love you.

Kathy Bleichrodt, my soul sister, for the gift of lifelong friendship and so much more.

Kem Lutz and *Alice Hammond*, for loving hearts, strong shoulders, and ready ears.

Beth Sigg, for reminding me who I am, and for the *M* and *J* coffee mugs.

My attorney, *George Simpson*, for refusing to let me give up without a fight.

Crista McIntosh, for the countless times you listened to me rant, shared my tears, and kept me sane. Some days you were my lifeline.

My coworkers, for giving me a sense of stability and normalcy when nothing else did.

Leverne Pfile, for helping me through some very difficult times. Though you retired before my divorce, I still drew on your wise counsel to get through this AFGE. You truly are a gift from God.

Susan McIntosh, Deacon Bob Angelich, our divorce support group, and all the courageous women and men I've met through this ministry. I'm sorry divorce is our common denominator, but I'm grateful our paths crossed. Thank you for your honesty, encouragement, friendship, and vision. You inspire me.

Allison Mayer, for your friendship, your candor, and your trust.

Nancy Erickson, The Book Professor®, whose expertise and process helped bring this book from concept to reality. Your friendship is icing on the cake. (Oops, sorry for the cliché.)

About the Author

ODDLY ENOUGH, Mary Jo "MJ" Rennert's eclectic career path prepared her to write this book. A registered nurse by education, she also painted portraits and worked in the publishing industry for ten years as an art director, editor, and writer. She completed the Diocese of Fort Wayne–South Bend's Education for Ministry Program and served her parish as a pastoral minister and parish nurse before launching a family-owned business.

Along the way, Mary Jo studied Pope (now Saint) John Paul II's *Theology of the Body* and wrote about the beauty and sanctity of married love. After her divorce, she completed Grief Recovery Method® (GRM) Specialist training through the Grief Recovery Institute®. Both *Theology of the Body* and GRM influence her approach to divorce recovery.

Mary Jo was married for forty-four years and has two adult children and one granddaughter. She wrote this book under her maiden name.

Mary Jo is passionate about divorce ministry and views it as an urgent need in the Church at large. She's available for retreats and days of reflection and can be contacted via her website, www.maryjorennert.com. Readers can find her blog there, along with helpful free resources.

www.ingramcontent.com/pod-product-compliance
Lightning Source LLC
Chambersburg PA
CBHW071355080526
44587CB00017B/3114